Standing FIRM

A CHRISTIAN RESPONSE TO HOSTILITY AND PERSECUTION

Standing FIRM

A CHRISTIAN RESPONSE TO HOSTILITY AND PERSECUTION

Jesse Yow

CONCORDIA PUBLISHING HOUSE · SAINT LOUIS

Published by Concordia Publishing House
3558 S. Jefferson Ave., St. Louis, MO 63118–3968
1-800-325-3040 • www.cph.org

Cover art: iStockphoto.com; Thinkstock

Manufactured in the United States of America

Library of Congress Cataloging-in-Publication Data

Yow, Jesse.

Standing firm : a Christian response to hostility and persecution / Jesse Yow.

pages cm

ISBN 978-0-7586-4921-8

1. Persecution. 2. Violence--Religious aspects--Christianity. 3. Hostility (Psychology) I. Title.

BR1601.3.Y69 2015

272'.9--dc23   2015023291

1   2   3   4   5   6   7   8   9   10   24   23   22   21   20   19   18   17   16   15

Table of Contents

Foreword

Persecution is a fact of life for millions of Christians across the globe. The most obvious (and horrifying) example is the extermination of Christians and destruction of Arab and African Christian communities in places dominated by groups such as the Islamic State in Syria and Iraq and Boko Haram in Nigeria. Even beyond this, amidst more moderate regimes across the Muslim world, Christians (and other non-Muslims) are prohibited from publicly expressing their faith and oftentimes harassed by civil authorities or molested by zealous mobs and individuals. Christians are persecuted not just by Muslim societies though. North Korea routinely arrests Christians and executes pastors. In neighboring China, where the Church is viewed as a threat to the state, it is constantly targeted for intimidation. And the list could go on, but this should not come as a surprise.

Christianity has often been viewed with suspicion and as a threat to the socio-political order. Just two decades after Jesus' ascension, for example, complaints were raised against the apostles and their companions because the message they proclaimed had "turned the world upside down" (Acts 17:6). It certainly did turn the pagan world upside down. To Greeks and Romans, Christians preached "foreign divinities" (Acts 17:18) and acted "against the decrees of Caesar" (Acts 17:7). The Roman historian Tacitus (AD 56–117) wrote that, for such reasons, they were regarded as "a class hated for their abominations." So Nero, the fifth emperor of Rome (AD 54 to AD 68), used them as a scapegoat to blame for the fire that devastated Rome in the summer of 64—a fire he may have ordered himself. An "immense multitude" of Christians were subsequently arrested, convicted, and summarily executed. Some were crucified. Others were wrapped in the pelts of animals and mauled to pieces by wild dogs. Still others were set on fire and used as human lanterns to illuminate the streets of Rome.[1]

This was the first but not necessarily the worst of the persecutions in the ancient world. The following two and a half centuries witnessed occasional (and sometimes frequent) outbursts of political and legally mandated violence directed at Christians. It all culminated in the great persecution under

---

1   Tacitus, *Annals*, 15.44.

Emperor Diocletian (ruled 284–305) beginning in 303. Bibles as well as places of worship were systematically destroyed. Christians were deprived of their rights and removed from political and military offices. Slaves who had once been legitimately freed were enslaved again. And in many parts, Christians were exterminated—the preferred method being burning the victims alive.

Something remarkable happened, though, in the wake of all this. After Diocletian's resignation from office in 305, the persecution of Christians diminished, and slowly Christianity began to be tolerated. The most famous—though by no means only—official move toward this was the issuing of the Edict of Milan in 313 by Emperor Constantine (ruled 306–337), which protected Christians by law for the first time. Certainly the status of Christians did not change everywhere overnight, but by and large the fourth century marked the beginning of the Christian centuries in the Mediterranean world.

Christianity eventually achieved dominance in the east. The overwhelming majority of the population became Christian; government, politics, and law followed suit. There was little to no distinction between church, state, and society. It took a little longer and certainly a different synthesis was achieved in the west, but by the time of Charlemagne (reigned 768–814), Christian civilization was well established on and beyond the boundaries of the Greco-Roman world. Although a good portion of its land to the east was occupied and its population subjugated under Islam in the seventh and eighth centuries, it persisted through the Middle Ages and into modernity.

The persecution of Christianity outside of western civilization might not come as a surprise. What is entirely surprising is the slow, subtle rise of persecution in the historically Christian, western world that was shaped by Christianity. To be sure, it pales in comparison to what is going on from Morocco to Pakistan, throughout China and elsewhere in the Far East. Nonetheless, it seems the west has entered—and has been in—what some are calling a post-Constantinian age, an age where certainly the privileges and perhaps the protection of orthodox Christianity are no longer legally guaranteed. Some are even suggesting that Christianity may someday soon find itself no longer tolerated.

There are a number of movements advocating for Christianity's marginalization if not its extinction. Author Sam Harris proudly argued for this in his New York Times bestseller, *The End of Faith* (New York: W. W. Norton and Company, 2005). Plenty of other influential intellectuals also confess to using their influence to deconstruct Christianity. Richard Rorty (1931–2007), for example, once explained how he used the classrooms of such prestigious institutions as Princeton and Stanford Universities to ridicule Christianity in order to strengthen the case for his own secular philosophy. In his view, Christian perspectives did not even deserve any sort of representation; he did not think they should even be tolerated in educated discourse.[2]

Opinions like these are certainly alarming, and they greatly contribute to the growing hostility toward Christianity. However, the real persecution Christians will face in the future will be much more formal. It will come from the state, will challenge the Church legally and financially, and will be driven by an ideological secularism. It is already happening. Although it might be temporary, it could—and probably will—grow increasingly worse. Whatever the case, this book will be helpful to navigate the future. *Standing Firm* carefully defines persecution and assesses its various manifestations around the globe before going on to consider the various causes and Christian responses to it. It leaves no stone unturned and covers every conceivable angle. Its author, Dr. Jesse Yow, has done a tremendous service for the Church as it stands poised ready to face the challenges of the foreseeable future.

Dr. Adam S. Francisco
Associate Professor of History and Political Thought
Concordia University Irvine

---

2   Richard Rorty, "Universality and Truth," in *Rorty and His Critics*, ed. Robert B. Brandom (Oxford: Blackwell, 2000), 21–22.

Acknowledgments

Writing a book like this starts slowly but at a deliberate pace, like starting a long cross-country race. As research informs the writing, some of the initial ideas fall by the wayside, other ideas evolve, and yet others grow and ferment. Nevertheless, the race proceeds and finds its own stride. As the Introduction suggests, one question leads to others, and every answer generates its own set of thoughts until the problem becomes one of keeping the scope of work in focus and limited to a manageable size. That is, running the race requires discipline and the ability to stay on the path. And even though the writing may start slowly, the pace quickens as more information comes to light and as thoughts and perspectives mature. By the end, writing moves forward at a furious pace, like a sprint to the finish line. And then it is done, with the satisfaction of having met the challenge!

I could not have finished this race on my own, so I would like to acknowledge the help and influence of several people who encouraged, endured, or supported me along the way. First, I need to humbly acknowledge and thank my wife, Dorcas, for her patience and prayer support. She ran interference and sacrificed her own time and energy to make my time more productive. She also cheered me on and served as a sounding board, always urging me to take a practical rather than abstract approach. Next, I would like to express my deep gratitude to Robert Newton, President of the Lutheran Church—Missouri Synod's California-Nevada-Hawaii District, for inspiration and encouragement. Iron sharpens iron, as Proverbs 27:17 so rightly observes, and Bob repeatedly sharpened my thinking. Then I would like to thank the brothers and sisters at Our Savior Lutheran Church in Livermore, California, who encouraged me and prayed for me throughout the race. I would like to highlight my appreciation for Laura Lane at Concordia Publishing House, who entertained the original proposal for writing this book, provided valuable feedback during the writing process, and then turned the draft manuscript into something useful. And finally, I thank and praise God for guiding, compelling, and sustaining me. Truly, He is faithful.

In His service,
Jesse Yow
Soli Deo Gloria!

Introduction

A simple question led to this book: if we Christians encounter hostility or persecution, what can we do besides turn the other cheek? This seemingly simple question gave rise to several more: How do we know if we have run into hostility because we are Christian or because someone is just having a bad day? When does hostility shade into oppression or persecution? Can such things even be happening in the United States? If so, how does our situation in the United States compare with that of Christians in other countries? And, to circle back to the original question, we all know that Jesus told us to turn the other cheek. What does God expect of us, and how would He like to use us in these challenging situations?

On one hand, in Matthew 5:39–41, Jesus states, "I say to you, Do not resist the one who is evil. But if anyone slaps you on the right cheek, turn to him the other also. And if anyone would sue you and take your tunic, let him have your cloak as well. And if anyone forces you to go one mile, go with him two miles." On the other hand, Jesus clearly challenges us to stand firm in the face of difficulties, trials, and opposition. In Mark 13:9, He declares, "But be on your guard. For they will deliver you over to councils, and you will be beaten in synagogues, and you will **stand** before governors and kings for My sake, to bear witness before them." The Epistles expand His guidance. For example, 1 Corinthians 16:13 urges us, "Be watchful, **stand firm** in the faith, act like men, be strong," and Galatians 5:1 urges,

"For freedom Christ has set us free; **stand firm** therefore, and do not submit again to a yoke of slavery." Perhaps most strikingly, Ephesians 6:10–13 adds to our understanding and exhorts,

> Finally, be strong in the Lord and in the strength of His might. Put on the whole armor of God, that you may be able to **stand** against the schemes of the devil. For we do not wrestle against flesh and blood, but against the rulers, against the authorities, against the cosmic powers over this present darkness, against the spiritual forces of evil in the heavenly places. Therefore take up the whole armor of God, that you may be able to with-**stand** in the evil day, and having done all, to **stand firm**.

The image is one of us receiving strength from God to be able to tenaciously submit to His will, glorify His name, and bear witness in all circumstances; this is not the image of a wimp or a doormat!

So when we encounter difficulties, trials, or opposition, what options might we have under the guidance of God's Word, and what are the implications? Note that we say *when* rather than *if*, and since you have read this far, you probably already suspected as much. This book wrestles with these questions and provides scriptural answers. The scope of such a study holds enough challenges of its own, so we will focus on the questions at hand rather than spending too much time on related topics in current geopolitical events or cultural changes. And even though it is very tempting to veer off into a debate about politics, national policies, or Americanized Christianity, we will save that discussion for another day and another venue. Our focus here is simply to explore that original question and some related derivative questions from a biblical foundation and in the broad context of current challenges.

Hostility and persecution against Christians seem to be growing in the United States and, with a few exceptions, in other countries worldwide. The U.S. has been trending in this direction for years as the nation becomes more secular and as Christianity's influence on culture and society wanes. Thus, Christians in North America face increasing pressure to keep their faith to themselves—to practice Christianity in private and not speak of

Jesus in public. Such pressure affects churches as well as individuals. It comes through covert or overt censorship, claims that speaking God's Word constitutes hate speech, accusations of hypocrisy and bigotry, and similar forms of hostility. These trends seem to have gone further and perhaps in a slightly different direction in Europe, where Christians face opposition from religious institutions[3] and secular organizations alike, and state churches often stand nearly empty as relics from when Christianity thrived.[4] Even worse, in a wide swath of the rest of the world, Christians face active persecution—including physical abuse, eviction, exile, imprisonment, and even death—because of their faith. Some might assume that conditions have always been this bad, but in fact more Christians are under siege today for their faith than even during the Roman persecution of the Early Church.[5]

What options do Christians have to respond to hostility or persecution, other than turning the other cheek? Such a question may seem speculative, even academic, until you experience hostility because of your faith or until some form of persecution comes to your community. Then the matter becomes personal and timely. Yet the whole matter is already personal and timely because many of our brothers and sisters in the faith face these challenges now. These people are our family in Christ, and we suffer as they suffer.

This book starts with a short overview of varieties of hostility and persecution taking place in North America, Europe, and the rest of the world. The situation is very fluid worldwide, with new developments turning up in reliable news accounts almost every day. Given the magnitude, complexity, and dynamic nature of the issues, we cannot catalog the whole picture nor provide a comprehensive report of political, geopolitical, or religious developments. For that kind of information, use the resources listed in the footnotes and in Appendix 1, and stay abreast of reliable news sources.

Instead of focusing completely on persecution *per se*, we will explore a sampling of recent and current events and see what we can learn from

---

3   Samuli Siikavirta, "Church of Finland Defrocks Dean Juhana Pohjola," International Lutheran Council, www.ilc-online.org, August 8, 2014.

4   Naftali Bendavid, "Europe's Empty Churches Go on Sale," *The Wall Street Journal*, January 2, 2015.

5   Morgan Lee, "Pope: More Persecuted Christians Today Than Ever Before," *The Christian Post*, July 1, 2014.

their patterns and common threads. Sometimes, the hostility directly confronts the faithful while at other times it is not clear that Christian faith provoked the hostility, so we will consider whether this question is a helpful distinction or just a distraction. Then we will drill down past appearances to explore the nature and roots of hostility against God's people as well as the basis for our response. We will use examples from the Old and New Testaments in our investigations so that we can begin to see how God works in such situations and frame the underlying theological principles. Such an approach will also help us maintain a practical view rather than straying off into abstractions. With this theological foundation in mind, we will next review what God's Word has to say about our approach to the problem, lay out the spiritual disciplines we need as a foundation for our response, and then identify biblical options for passive or active tactics that we can adapt to our situation. Finally, we will outline criteria for making our choices by looking at their implications for Christian witness and the Gospel. In the appendices, we will identify resources for further information, highlight some useful prayers and psalms to set examples for our own prayer life, and list a number of helpful Bible verses for quick reference. For a downloadable Bible study, visit cph.org/standingfirm.

You probably fall into one or more of these groups of readers: (1) those now experiencing hostility; (2) those who would support or encourage the afflicted; (3) those who would counsel, guide, or advise the afflicted; or (4) those who have not yet encountered hostility or paid much attention, but who are maybe looking into the topic for the first time. Regardless of which category might describe you, it is rather easy to talk about something in the abstract, but more difficult and much more useful to consider how it might involve or apply to you. To help you come to grips with hostility before it comes to grips with you, I urge you to consider the discussion questions and points for consideration provided at the end of each chapter. It would be particularly valuable to try to visualize how different situations might look. For example, what would invoking your legal rights actually involve, and what repercussions or difficulties might arise?

What can you do, or what should you do, after you read this book? I pray that you will recognize hostility against Christians for what it is, regardless of appearances; see the needs and opportunities to respond; and understand your options and responsibilities for taking action. Our choices certainly shape how we support our brethren and how we deal with our own situations, but in the end they dramatically affect our confession of faith. It is not too much to say that our witness to the Gospel of Christ is at stake, so I pray that this book encourages, informs, and challenges you on the path ahead!

⌘⌘

1

What's the Situation?

When we think of hostility or persecution directed toward Christians, many of us think of violence or death. We see violence in the headlines, though sometimes the news reports do not tell us that Christians were the target, and often they completely neglect the spiritual dimensions of the conflict. It is a misconception, though, to think that hostility and persecution must always involve bloodshed or death. In North America, hostility and persecution usually take on different forms: bullying, political correctness, censorship, or intimidation. The opposition may be subtle or obvious, and it may be personal and focused or more broadly aimed at entire classes or groups of people. The variety of situations and circumstances, coupled with the lack of extreme violence that we hear about in other parts of the world, can give rise to confusion about whether what we experience is truly opposition or if it has anything to do with our Christianity.

There will always be unanswered questions, but an open-minded review of the past few years of news reports reveals that Christians in the United States and Canada often encounter hostility in many different sectors of life, including in academia, in government, online, and in the workplace. The hostility may take any of several different forms, and sometimes its appearance can be misleading. Therefore, we may not always understand the situations we encounter or how we should best respond. Recent examples include a variety of instances such as these:

- Gay-rights activists publish the names of people who contribute toward a legislative initiative supporting heterosexual marriage, and people in high-visibility jobs encounter a public smear campaign when their names appear on the list. Christians on the list wonder, *"Is this persecution, or am I being too sensitive? What should I do?"*[1]

- Teenage vandals break into a church late one night, overturn the piano, trash a classroom, and turn on a fire hose to flood the floor. Inspecting the damage, the pastor and parishioners wonder if they had been singled out for a hate crime, or if this was just kids "acting out." *What should they say when interviewed by a local reporter?*[2]

- Demonstrators invade a worship service, shouting slogans against the pastor and congregation for teaching biblical moral values and speaking of forgiveness from sin. *How should the church handle this hostility?*[3]

- Secular activists pressure a social media company to block posts that carry a Christian perspective because Christian views are "divisive," "discriminatory," and "hate-filled." Since social media provide platforms for public communication, does such a secular vigilante movement infringe on freedom of speech? Since it does not affect a particular individual or congregation, but only a

---

1   Declaration of John Doe 2 in Support of Plaintiffs' Motion for Summary Judgment, ProtectMarriage.com v. Bowen, No. 2:09-cv-00058 (E.D. Cal. filed Jan. 15, 2009); (Exhibit A).

2   "Three teenagers arrested for repeatedly vandalizing church," *San Francisco Chronicle*, November 14, 1996.

3   "Gay activists disrupt Sunday service at Michigan church," *Catholic News Agency*, November 13, 2008.

broad class of people, is this kind of censorship even an issue? *If so, how should Christians respond?*[4]

These difficult situations raise questions about the rule of law and civil liberties such as freedoms of speech, assembly, and religion. More significantly, they have implications regarding the credibility of our public witness, opportunities to share the Gospel of Jesus Christ, and how our antagonists and bystanders perceive Christians and God.

It seems inevitable that Christians, the Church, and the Gospel of Christ will encounter hostility or other negative behavior. In fact, looking back over the past two millennia of Church history, periods of peace were always interrupted sooner or later by times of persecution. Or was it that periods of persecution were punctuated by times of peace? Regardless, hostility should not come as a surprise. After all, our Lord warned in John 15:19, "If you were of the world, the world would love you as its own; but because you are not of the world, but I chose you out of the world, therefore the world hates you." Recall that our Lord came into this world to save it, knowing full well that He would encounter hostility that would climax at the cross. He chose us out of the world, yet leaves us here for a time as His ambassadors, knowing we will encounter hostility as we follow Him. In John 10:14–15, Jesus says, "I am the good shepherd. I know My own and My own know Me, just as the Father knows Me and I know the Father; and I lay down My life for the sheep." We respond in faith, worshiping Him as Romans 12:1 urges: "Present your bodies as a living sacrifice, holy and acceptable to God, which is your spiritual worship." He laid down His life for us once for all time; we offer our lives for Him as an ongoing, living sacrifice. This sets the stage for our life as His people.

> "Because you are not of the world, but I chose you out of the world, therefore the world hates you." (John 15:19)

---

4   Tiffany Owens, "Rocky future for freedom on social media," *WORLD News Group*, February 28, 2013, and Whitney Williams, "Twitter mutes pro-life group ahead of rally," *WORLD News Group*, February 14, 2013.

Is It Truly Persecution?

When we do encounter hostility, we need to take a clear-eyed approach to discerning some things about the situation so that we can respond appropriately and correctly rather than react from emotion or false premises. First, if we are blessed to live in a country that values free speech and open exchange of ideas, are we really encountering hostility or is someone just disagreeing with us? Christianity wins in the competition of ideas, but the competition itself can sometimes be bruising. Disagreement is not the same as hostility, opposition, or persecution. Second, have we done something that warrants punishment, such as breaking God's Law as reflected in civil law? First Peter 4:14–15 states, "If you are insulted for the name of Christ, you are blessed, because the Spirit of glory and of God rests upon you. But let none of you suffer as a murderer or a thief or an evildoer or as a meddler." Romans 13:3–4 completes the picture:

> For rulers are not a terror to good conduct, but to bad. Would you have no fear of the one who is in authority? Then do what is good, and you will receive his approval, for he is God's servant for your good. But if you do wrong, be afraid, for he does not bear the sword in vain. For he is the servant of God, an avenger who carries out God's wrath on the wrongdoer.

Scripture clearly warns that we should not be surprised if we suffer for doing something wrong, so we must not think that punishment for crime is the same as persecution.

What if after careful consideration we realize that what is happening to us is more than the competition of ideas on a level playing field, and not prompted by criminal behavior on our part? Then who is it that opposes or shows hostility toward Christians? Are they individuals, a group of some sort, or an organization? Are they hostile only toward Christians, or toward those in other religions as well? Finally, does our situation involve random, one-of-a-kind events such as robbery or vandalism, or is it systematic, repeated, or pervasive? Is the hostility driven by ideology or belief systems, or does it reflect some other cause, such as greed, fear, or some kind of honest misunderstanding?

The questions framed above provide filters to help discern if our circumstances actually reflect hostility toward Christians or the Church—a hostility that attempts to block the Gospel of Christ—or if it is something else. Their answers affect our options for response, and possibly whether we need to respond at all. This scrutiny in no way denies or diminishes the reality of hostility targeting Christians, but it does help our understanding. We do not want to be guilty of crying wolf when there is no wolf of persecution at the door. On the other hand, if the wolf really is at the door, we need to sound the alert and think through how we will respond.

Scripture makes it clear that God's people, sanctified and secure in God's grace, are also dispersed as ambassadors of the Gospel according to His will.[5] In other words, God deliberately places Christians where He wants them to witness, minister, and serve. Therefore, our individual situations are not accidental, random events. We should not be taken by surprise when we run into hostility but should look at our circumstances as opportunities to stand together, draw closer to God, and point a fallen world toward our Lord and Savior, Jesus Christ. And we should know that God has placed us there, rather than assuming that our difficult situation has somehow escaped His notice.

Living in this reality, we can expect that Christians, the Church, and the Gospel will rarely encounter neutrality, but will often run into a variety of negative behaviors. We can sort these behaviors into different levels to help sketch out the problem, establish a common understanding of different types of behavior, and provide a basis for discernment to help avoid overreacting or underreacting as we respond.

Hostility, opposition, and persecution are not tidy, discrete categories, because they are somewhat overlapping terms. They represent shades of gray, ranging from thoughts to words to deeds, based on how the hostility is expressed and perhaps reflecting the goal or intent of the hostile behavior. The shades of gray, then, may begin with some degree of indifference or *apathy* toward Christians, the Church, or the Gospel. As *hostility* begins to arise, Christians may become targets of negative behavior expressed

---

5 First Peter 1:1 describes Christians as "elect exiles of the Dispersion." The Greek root word for "Dispersion," *diaspora,* is also the root for our word *spore. Spore* points to our role as seeds, moved by God's Spirit to wherever He wills, and *elect* emphasizes that we are chosen and placed according to God's sovereign purpose.

by written or spoken words in public settings, such as community functions, legal proceedings, or government processes. This level of behavior might best be described as a form of bullying. As hostility grades into **opposition**, though, Christians may encounter attempts to intimidate, stop, or block their witness or civil freedoms of speech, assembly, or religion. This could include activity (e.g., threats, slander, libel, or violence) intended to marginalize, eliminate, or delegitimize the Christian message. As hostility transitions into *persecution*, Christians will face attempts to eliminate their witness or freedoms of speech, assembly, or religion. Opponents will seek out or pursue Christians with such attacks and will try to keep Christians on the defensive in an attempt to prevent any proactive response. This will probably include activity (including intimidation or violence) intended not only to stop the Gospel message but also to marginalize, dehumanize, or eliminate Christians themselves.

As hostility and opposition intensify, the behavior becomes more personal, more active, and more aimed at eliminating Christians along with their confession of God's Word. Note also that we are describing behaviors based on their opposition to Christians and God's Word without any explicit mention of underlying motivations. This will help avoid tangential and potentially unhelpful arguments about whether bullying or other bad behavior is or is not hostility against Christians. It is important to realize that the practical effects of hostility are to impede or stop Christian witness to or confession of the Gospel regardless of whether that is the apparent or claimed reason for the opposition. In fact, hostility may seem to arise from any of several different factors. For example, consider the opposition that arose in Acts 19:23–41, which relates,

> About that time there arose no little disturbance concerning the Way. For a man named Demetrius, a silversmith, who made silver shrines of Artemis, brought no little business to the craftsmen. These he gathered together, with the workmen in similar trades, and said, "Men, you know that from this business we have our wealth. And you see and hear that not only in Ephesus but in almost all of Asia this Paul has persuaded and turned away a great many people, saying that gods made with hands are not gods. And there is danger not only

that this trade of ours may come into disrepute but also that the temple of the great goddess Artemis may be counted as nothing, and that she may even be deposed from her magnificence, she whom all Asia and the world worship."

When they heard this they were enraged and were crying out, "Great is Artemis of the Ephesians!" So the city was filled with the confusion, and they rushed together into the theater, dragging with them Gaius and Aristarchus, Macedonians who were Paul's companions in travel. But when Paul wished to go in among the crowd, the disciples would not let him. And even some of the Asiarchs, who were friends of his, sent to him and were urging him not to venture into the theater. Now some cried out one thing, some another, for the assembly was in confusion, and most of them did not know why they had come together. Some of the crowd prompted Alexander, whom the Jews had put forward. And Alexander, motioning with his hand, wanted to make a defense to the crowd. But when they recognized that he was a Jew, for about two hours they all cried out with one voice, "Great is Artemis of the Ephesians!"

And when the town clerk had quieted the crowd, he said, "Men of Ephesus, who is there who does not know that the city of the Ephesians is temple keeper of the great Artemis, and of the sacred stone that fell from the sky? Seeing then that these things cannot be denied, you ought to be quiet and do nothing rash. For you have brought these men here who are neither sacrilegious nor blasphemers of our goddess. If therefore Demetrius and the craftsmen with him have a complaint against anyone, the courts are open, and there are proconsuls. Let them bring charges against one another. But if you seek anything further, it shall be settled in the regular assembly. For we really are in danger of being charged with rioting today, since there is no cause that we can give to justify this commotion." And when he had said these things, he dismissed the assembly.

Was this opposition to Christianity driven by economic, religious, personality, or other factors? It was apparently a combination of factors rather than someone simply deciding that they disliked Christians. Regardless, our central concern here revolves around the effect of hostility, how to understand it, and how to respond.

Hostility in North America

Compared to many other parts of the world, the United States remains an orderly society that lives under civil law with open exchange of ideas and constitutional guarantees of freedoms of religion, speech, and assembly. However, many have suggested that the U.S. has entered a post-Church, post-Christian age, citing the decline in the amount of people regularly attending worship services, the decline in numbers of people active in Christian churches, and apparent decline in the influence of Christianity on community, regional, and national cultural values. These trends reflect an evolution of social norms over many years, if not decades, with tangled cause-effect relationships underlying apparent trends. They represent changes in perspectives and values that contribute to lowering community standards for what is or is not acceptable behavior, so that actions once considered intolerable and out of bounds might now be seen as uninformed or even socially acceptable. In turn, this opens the door for increasing opposition, hostility, or persecution against Christians.

Opposition and hostility toward Christians occurs in a U.S. cultural context that has been drifting for decades. The nation seems to be moving toward a new normal that is rather different and darker from what was considered normal for the first two centuries after the Declaration of Independence, Constitution, and Bill of Rights were written. Particularly over the generations since World War II, the Church has found itself increasingly distanced from American culture and society. America's post-Church, post-Christian views evolved through several stages, starting with apathy toward God and followed in succession by denial of absolute truth, loss of moral and ethical foundations, social approval of what was previously considered bad behavior, and then hostility toward those with faith that speak the truth.[6] It parallels the death spiral Paul described in Romans 1:21–32,

---

6   D. C. Innes, "Prepare yourself for cultural exile," *WORLD News Group*, August 11, 2014.

For although they knew God, they did not honor Him as God or give thanks to Him, but they became futile in their thinking, and their foolish hearts were darkened. Claiming to be wise, they became fools, and exchanged the glory of the immortal God for images resembling mortal man and birds and animals and creeping things.

Therefore **God gave them up** in the lusts of their hearts to impurity, to the dishonoring of their bodies among themselves, because they exchanged the truth about God for a lie and worshiped and served the creature rather than the Creator, who is blessed forever! Amen.

For this reason **God gave them up** to dishonorable passions. For their women exchanged natural relations for those that are contrary to nature; and the men likewise gave up natural relations with women and were consumed with passion for one another, men committing shameless acts with men and receiving in themselves the due penalty for their error.

And since they did not see fit to acknowledge God, **God gave them up** to a debased mind to do what ought not to be done. They were filled with all manner of unrighteousness, evil, covetousness, malice. They are full of envy, murder, strife, deceit, maliciousness. They are gossips, slanderers, haters of God, insolent, haughty, boastful, inventors of evil, disobedient to parents, foolish, faithless, heartless, ruthless. Though they know God's righteous decree that those who practice such things deserve to die, they not only do them but give approval to those who practice them.

Notice the common thread running through the passage: people turning away from God, rejecting God's truth, encouraging others to do likewise, and God punishing those people by simply giving them up to what they want. With this kind of unraveling of society, it is no wonder that Christians can expect more and more hostility. People who are hostile toward

> **People who are hostile toward God will naturally take out some of that hostility on His people.**

God will naturally take out some of that hostility on His people. Once we understand that our communities and social institutions suffer the kinds of spiritual decay Paul described, we can begin to recognize that hostile behavior toward Christians in North America may be more common than many people realize. Consider the examples of passive and active hostility that follow. Are any of them familiar to you?

- Violence that singles out Christians or churches as targets, including vandalism, protests or demonstrations that disrupt worship services, church invasion robberies, shootings, or other forms of violence[7]

- Public recognition, endorsement, or promotion of other belief systems or religions in order to appear non-discriminatory, especially when such support is not afforded equally to Christians

- Employment practices that discriminate in their hiring or employment policies according to religious belief[8]

- Offering or requiring classes and seminars on religions other than Christianity while excluding similar classes on Christianity

- Workplace practices such as providing prayer rooms for Muslims but not for Christians, or recognizing holidays for other religions but not for Christians (e.g., accommodating Ramadan for Muslims but not Lent for Christians)

---

7   "Gay activists disrupt Sunday service at Michigan church," *Catholic News Agency*, November 13, 2008.

8   Bradley R. E. Wright, "Your Faith Might Cost You Your Next Job," *ChristianityToday.com*, June 18, 2014.

- Preferential practices or discriminatory treatment in school or university settings, including denial of tenure to Christian professors, faculty intimidation of Christian students, denial of school facility use to Christian groups but opening facilities to other religious groups, or requiring Christian groups to accept non-Christians as leaders[9]

- Discrimination in government policies, including pressure on chaplains to conform to secular dogma on gender, sexuality, and morality; government attempts to redefine or redirect religious practices; and threats of fines, taxes, or penalties against religious belief or practice[10]

Recently the U.S. and Canada have begun experiencing two incremental developments that have a special impact on Christians and the Church: (1) portrayal of Christians, Christian beliefs, and the Bible as hateful and bigoted; and (2) attempts to limit Christians' constitutional freedoms of religion, speech, and assembly to a much narrower freedom of private worship. These trends have been incremental, proceeding in a series of small steps over the past few years, but will eventually have a cumulatively devastating effect on Christians and the Church if they continue unchecked.

Portrayal of Christians as hate-filled persecutors (e.g., with respect to homosexual marriage, euthanasia, or abortion) appears to be part of a broad attempt to marginalize Christians and remove their influence from American culture. Related developments include revoking accreditation of Christian schools,[11] eviction of Christian groups from university

---

9   Tom Krattenmaker, "Commentary: A Christian should lead Christians," *Reporter Online*, November 17, 2014; Josh Good, "The D-word is coming to a campus near you," *WORLD News Group*, October 11, 2014; and Sarah Padbury, "Colorado high school bans prayer meeting during 'free time,'" *WORLD News Group*, November 20, 2014.

10   Michael Cochrane, "Army chaplain reprimanded for discussing his faith," *WORLD News Group*, December 15, 2014; Patrick J. Reilly, "School Ground Bullies in the Nation's Capital," *The Wall Street Journal*, December 26, 2014; Courtney Crandell, "California: All health insurance must cover abortion," *WORLD News Group*, August 25, 2014; and Joy Pullmann, "For The West, Christian Hunting Is The Sport Of Lawmakers And Judges," *The Federalist*, December 29, 2014.

11   J. C. Derrick, "Canadian education minister revokes approval for Christian law school," *WORLD News Group*, December 12, 2014.

campuses,[12] demands that Christians who own and operate businesses implement policies that violate their conscience,[13] and demands for pastors to submit their sermons to civil authorities.[14] If successful, this broad movement seems likely to lead to denial of Christian access to communication channels (e.g., removing "objectionable" material from the Internet), political and judicial processes, and public discussion of competing ideas. These developments appear reminiscent of approaches used by some countries in the 1930s and 1940s to marginalize Jews before the subsequent onset of physical persecution. They also seem to spring up by an informal consensus rather than by coordinated plan, and they come from an element of society that has turned its back on Christianity and now finds itself offended by the Law and Gospel of Jesus Christ. In other words, it is driven by a common heritage of original sin.

In a more subtle kind of attack, rhetorical and political efforts to replace "freedom of religion" with "freedom of worship" seem to be an attempt to limit the freedom of Christians (as well as members of other faith communities) to practice their faith outside the confines of places of worship.[15] In a sense, worship then becomes only a private activity, because it is isolated from the surrounding community. More broadly, free expression of faith, Christian ministry, and sharing God's Word in the community at large would no longer be protected civil rights, meaning that the constitutional guarantees of the freedoms of religion, speech, and public assembly would effectively be denied to Christians.

Hostility in Europe

In other countries where Christianity is acceptable (e.g., most European and Latin American countries at this time), Christian witness is legal even if perhaps somewhat unpopular or out of favor. Christians are mostly

---

12 Josh Good, "The D-word is coming to a campus near you," *WORLD News Group*, October 11, 2014.

13 See Frank Bruni, "Your God and My Dignity: Religious Liberty, Bigotry and Gays," *New York Times*, January 10, 2015 in conjunction with James Taranto, "Call the Cake Police!," *The Wall Street Journal*, January 14, 2015.

14 Brian Lee, "Houston To Pastors: Turn Over Your Sermons," *The Federalist*, October 15, 2014.

15 Jonathan Imbody, "Obama 'freedom to worship' assaults First Amendment," *The Washington Times*, January 28, 2013.

tolerated in these countries, sometimes to the point of taking the Church for granted. Such a prevailing attitude may reflect apathy toward the Gospel, but an apathy that could easily shift into antipathy in the future. Indeed, the situation for Christian churches has been deteriorating in Europe, with many churches closing and others becoming part of state or secularized institutions.[16] In some cases, the antipathy has begun to show itself, as when a European state church takes steps to defrock pastors who would preach and teach from the Bible.[17] This creates a disturbing situation, where long-established denominations that claim to be Christian become opponents of orthodox Christian teaching and take action against pastors and members who remain faithful to God's revealed truth.

Observing these trends and developments, some have wondered if the United States and Canada will follow Europe into its particular style of secularization. North America certainly seems to be heading in a secular direction, but it is not clear that the U.S. will follow the same path as Europe. Many factors influence the evolution of a country's social fabric and culture, and demographic trends play a major role in each region's future. Over the past decade or more, Europe has seen a large influx of immigrants from across the Middle East as well as Africa and other areas, with a large proportion of these people coming from Muslim faith communities and ethnic groups. The U.S., by comparison, has seen immigration from various parts of Asia, Eastern Europe, and Latin America, with a large number of people coming from Catholic or Orthodox faith traditions. Meanwhile, the birthrates among non-immigrant portions of the population have been trending downward in both the U.S. and Europe. "Demographics are Destiny," as the saying goes, and these broad-brush observations suggest that the U.S. and Europe may not actually be on the same path in terms of religious climate and hostility toward Christians.

Barring a change in direction, the U.S. will likely become less and less hospitable toward both Christians and churches that speak God's truth. Secular rejection of absolute truth, government's embrace of political expediency

---

16 Naftali Bendavid, "Europe's Empty Churches Go on Sale," *The Wall Street Journal*, January 2, 2015.

17 Samuli Siikavirta, "Church of Finland Defrocks Dean Juhana Pohjola," International Lutheran Council, www.ilc-online.org, August 8, 2014; Esko Murto and Samuli Siikavirta, "Pastors defrocked by ELCF: We have not broken our ordination vows," The Evangelical Lutheran Mission Diocese of Finland, April 10, 2015.

rather than rule by law, and the growth of a multiculturalism that embraces all values and versions of truth as equal regardless of their validity or virtue all combine to fuel this trend away from God's truth. In this regard, the U.S. and Europe are on similar paths, but Europe is further down the road. On the other hand, much of the immigration into the U.S. is neutral or supports Christianity, while much of the immigration into Europe is apathetic toward or rejects Christianity.

God can surprise us.

These differences in how our populations are changing will make our paths diverge, but the trends need detailed study to more fully understand their implications. And don't forget that God can surprise us. Old Testament narratives show that He can turn a nation (even a pagan place like Nineveh, as Jonah witnessed) very quickly indeed if He chooses to do so.

Where Christians Have It Worse

The situation for Christians in many parts of the world is often worse than the apathy or hostility encountered in the United States or Europe.[18] In some other countries, Christian witness or even speaking of Jesus may be illegal, conversion to Christianity may be a criminal offense, and public displays of faith are repressed. Such a prevailing attitude of opposition is not as severe, though, as the persecution found in yet other countries, where Christians are imprisoned, tortured, enslaved, or murdered; churches are subject to terrorist attack; and, in some cases, churches are not allowed to exist except underground, out of sight of the persecutors. These countries are the darkest in terms of severity of persecution, in that the countries involved often try to conceal the persecution, and because publicity about Christians or Christian activity within such countries could trigger waves of additional oppression and reprisal.

The maps that follow show parts of the world in which Christians are persecuted. The first map simply shows a broad swath of the world where Christians are oppressed; the second map provides a visual representation of the severity of persecution. These situations are dynamic and may change from area to area and from year to year. Therefore, assessments of persecution may not be completely up to the minute with changing conditions, but they still reflect a good faith attempt to portray conditions in each country. This necessarily represents a subjective judgment since the governments involved in or allowing the persecution often censor or deny relevant information, including names, places, affiliations, and numbers of people involved or affected. Even if such information is not completely blocked, it may be filtered or go unreported by the U.S. government or by the news media, making it hard to verify any data or accounts that do become available.

---

18   "The Global Religion Crisis," *The Wall Street Journal*, July 31, 2014.

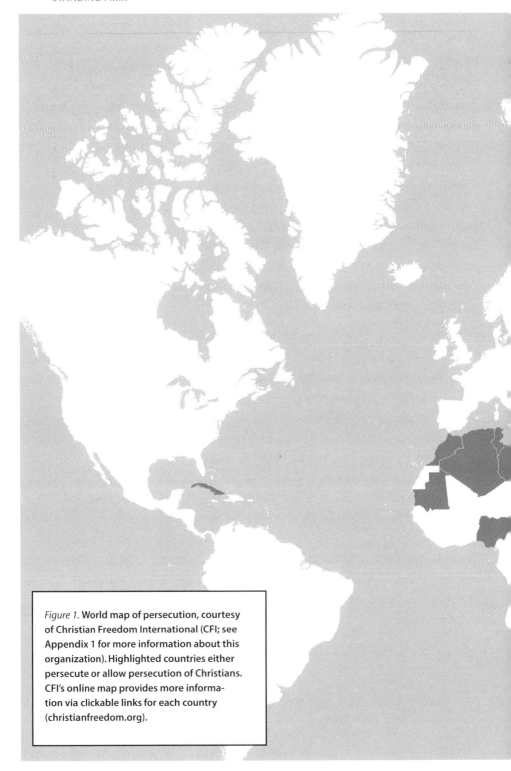

Figure 1. World map of persecution, courtesy of Christian Freedom International (CFI; see Appendix 1 for more information about this organization). Highlighted countries either persecute or allow persecution of Christians. CFI's online map provides more information via clickable links for each country (christianfreedom.org).

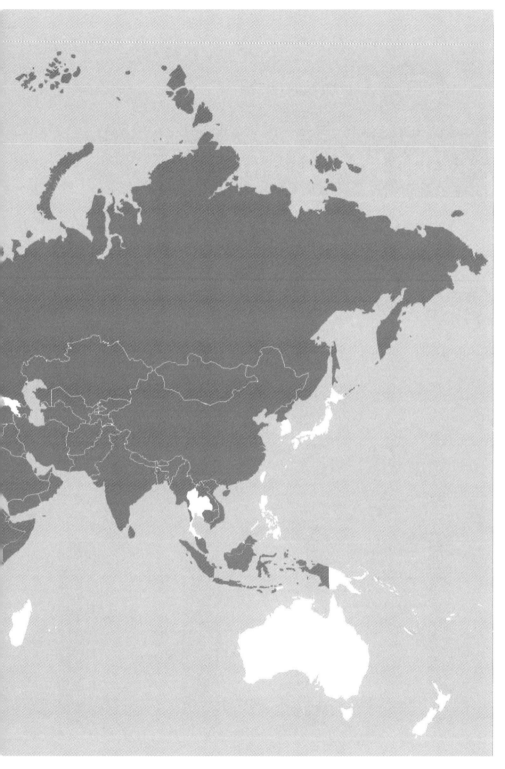

2015 WORLD WATCH LIST

The World Watch List is a ranking of the top 50 countries where the persecution of Christians is most severe.

Open Doors works in the world's most oppressive countries, strengthening Christians to stand strong in the face of persecution and equipping them to shine Christ's light in these places.

MEXICO

ALGER

MAURITANIA MALI

COLOMBIA

	Extreme Persecution	4	Syria	11	Maldives	18	Qatar
	Severe Persecution	5	Afghanistan	12	Saudi Arabia	19	Kenya
	Moderate Persecution	6	Sudan	13	Libya	20	Turkmenistan
	Sparse Persecution	7	Iran	14	Yemen	21	India
1	North Korea	8	Pakistan	15	Uzbekistan	22	Ethiopia
2	Somalia	9	Eritrea	16	Vietnam	23	Egypt
3	Iraq	10	Nigeria	17	Central African Republic	24	Djibouti

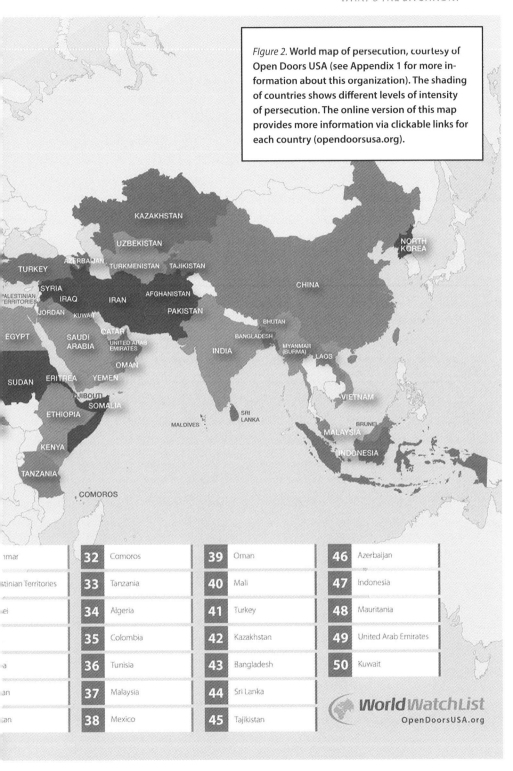

Figure 2. World map of persecution, courtesy of Open Doors USA (see Appendix 1 for more information about this organization). The shading of countries shows different levels of intensity of persecution. The online version of this map provides more information via clickable links for each country (opendoorsusa.org).

ımar	**32**	Comoros	**39**	Oman	**46**	Azerbaijan
tinian Territories	**33**	Tanzania	**40**	Mali	**47**	Indonesia
ei	**34**	Algeria	**41**	Turkey	**48**	Mauritania
	35	Colombia	**42**	Kazakhstan	**49**	United Arab Emirates
a	**36**	Tunisia	**43**	Bangladesh	**50**	Kuwait
an	**37**	Malaysia	**44**	Sri Lanka		
an	**38**	Mexico	**45**	Tajikistan		

WorldWatchList
OpenDoorsUSA.org

Differences between the two maps reflect the results of trying to assess and portray levels of persecution based on data that will always be incomplete and in transition. In terms of our earlier sorting of hostility into four somewhat overlapping levels (apathy, hostility, opposition, and persecution), the shaded areas of each map represent widespread opposition or persecution; the other, non-highlighted areas of each map generally represent areas where Christians encounter apathy or some degree of hostility.

The first map, from Christian Freedom International, compiles information from the U.S. Commission on International Religious Freedom (USCIRF) "countries of concern" list; the second map, from Open Doors USA, reflects a "top-50" country list. Both maps are correct according to the information and assumptions used to create them; both maps are useful because of the information and insights that they provide. Differences emerge where countries show up highlighted on one map but not the other. For example, the CFI map highlights Russia, Cuba, and Nepal (reflecting the hostility of communist and Maoist belief systems toward Christianity), but the Open Doors map does not. The Open Doors map highlights Mexico, Colombia, and Mali (representing diverse sources of hostility, but not really a single major influence like Communism), while the CFI map does not.

As we have noted, the maps can change from year to year because the situation in each country can be dynamic. A nation that was once flagged because of persecution might embrace religious freedom, putting an end to persecution and causing a change in its status. Or, of course, conditions might go the other direction and put a nation back in the "highlighted" category. Studying and comparing the maps leads to further insights:

- Government-sponsored or government-allowed persecution of Christians tends to occur in a wide strip of countries that have either predominantly Muslim or Hindu populations or whose authoritarian governments try to enforce an atheist mindset. In fact, this applies to most of the highlighted countries on both maps.

- Some differences may reflect a transition in a country's behavior or simply a judgment call regarding how pervasive or severe the persecution is in that country. For example, Christian witness and the opportunity to change from one religion to another were both outlawed in Nepal for years. In addition, Maoists in that country opposed Christianity as a matter of policy driven by their communist belief system. Recently, though, a few high-profile Nepalese have come forward to confess faith in Christ and at least one government agency has begun speaking of religious freedom, so the situation may be changing for the better.[19] Thus, Nepal shows up as prone to oppress Christians on one map but not on the other.

- Geopolitical processes can change the maps as extremist movements operate across borders and attempt to overthrow existing nations. For example, the Islamic State is making war across parts of Syria and Iraq, and Boko Haram is fighting across northern Nigeria and into the neighboring nation of Cameroon. As explained below, both of these Muslim movements persecute Christians as well as less extreme Muslims and members of other religions. Further, both groups apparently aim to redraw national borders as they establish new caliphates in their respective parts of the world.

As mentioned above, the maps reflect trouble for Christians in a wide swath of countries around the world. Persecution can be triggered by accusations of blasphemy against Allah or Muhammad, by false charges of mishandling the Qur'an, or by any number of other sometimes seemingly innocuous events.[20] Certain areas deserve special mention, though: the Middle East, west central Africa, south central Asia, and eastern/northeastern Asia.

---

19 See Julia A. Seymour, "Christianity's growth in Nepal includes celebrity convert," *WORLD News Group*, October 6, 2014; Julia A. Seymour, "Religious minorities find a voice in Indonesia, Nepal," *WORLD News Group*, November 17, 2014.

20 See "Blasphemy in Pakistan: Bad-mouthing," *The Economist*, November 29, 2014.

Middle East

The number of Christians in the Middle East is dwindling because of pressures from Islamic aggression in parallel with a lack of government protection for religious freedom.[21] In many cases, Middle Eastern governments operate under constitutions based on Islamic law and do not offer the level of civil rights and protections found in the United States, Canada, or much of Europe. Christians are a religious minority in Middle Eastern countries, and vulnerable.

Some nations, such as Saudi Arabia, oppress Christians by treating the Bible as a banned book, outlawing evangelism, prohibiting religious conversion, and preventing Christians from establishing churches for public worship. Other nations are more violent toward Christians. For example, the Christian church in Baghdad tries to persevere[22] and even tries to shelter a smaller minority of Jews. Yet with frequent bombings and other violence against churches and their members, it is not clear how long they can hold out.[23] Similar kinds of oppression of Christians and churches can be found in most other Muslim countries across the region.

Although it is not a nation per se, the self-proclaimed Islamic State has taken over large parts of Syria and Iraq by force and is threatening neighboring countries such as Saudi Arabia, Jordan, and Lebanon. When Islamic State forces first take over an area, they mark homes and businesses of Christians with this symbol:

Arabic character for "N" used by Islamic State militants to mark Christian homes and businesses for further attention (e.g., eviction or destruction). The character "N" stands for Nazarene, in reference to Jesus of Nazareth.

Christians in areas conquered by the Islamic State typically face a choice of converting to Islam at gunpoint, paying the jizya (a tax demanded of non-Muslims, like paying protection money to a local gang), execution, or leaving the area.[24] The mark on their property helps ensure

---

21 See Philip Jenkins, "Is This the End for Mideast Christianity?" *Christianity Today*, November 4, 2014.

22 See Maria Abi-Habib, "Iraq's Christian Minority Feels Militant Threat," *The Wall Street Journal*, June 26, 2014.

23 See Mindy Belz, "The Edge of Extinction," *WORLD News Group*, May 17, 2014.

24 See Tamara Audi, "Iraqi Christians' Dilemma: Stay or Go?" *The Wall Street Journal*, September 29,

that they won't be missed when Islamic State enforcers sweep back through the neighborhood.

Central Africa

Looking south to central Africa, a militant Islamic group known as Boko Haram has taken control of much of northeast Nigeria and has begun to spill over into neighboring countries such as Cameroon.[25] Boko Haram, whose name translates into English as something roughly like "Western education is sacrilege," has been working hard to purge the area of Christians and any others who do not embrace their fundamentalist version of Islam.[26] Their goal seems to be creation of a new Islamic state, or Caliphate, which they will rule by Shariah law.[27] Early in 2014, the group kidnapped almost three hundred schoolgirls, most of them Christian, and reportedly forced them to convert to Islam or sold them into slavery.[28] Observers estimate that Boko Haram killings numbered into the low thousands in 2014 alone, and the persecution and purging continue as the group recently destroyed at least sixteen villages and towns in northern Nigeria, killing many and forcing others to flee across the border into Chad.[29]

Southern Asia

Turning east toward southern Asia, we find persecution of Christians in Afghanistan and Pakistan, and Hindu oppression of both Muslims and Christians in India. Muslim persecution of Christians in Pakistan includes the ubiquitous abuse of blasphemy laws[30] and, more recently, the massacre

---

2014; Leslie Loftis, "Don't Close Your Eyes To Christians Purged And Tortured in Iraq," *The Federalist*, August 1, 2014; and Rob Schwarzwalder, "Who Is Speaking For The Persecuted Christians in Iraq?," *The Federalist*, August 15, 2014.

25 See Julia A. Seymour, "Boko Haram expanding from Nigeria to Cameroon," *WORLD News Group*, September 22, 2014.

26 See Drew Hinshaw and Gbenga Akingbule, "Boko Haram Rampages, Slaughters in Northeast Nigeria," *The Wall Street Journal*, January 9, 2015.

27 See "Islamic State of Northern Nigeria," *The American Interest*, November 16, 2014.

28 See Jamie Dean, "The Lost Girls," *WORLD News Group*, May 31, 2014, and J. C. Derrick, "U.S. Official: Boko Haram isn't targeting just Christians," *WORLD News Group*, May 21, 2014.

29 See Jamie Dean, "Nigeria attack: Too many bodies to count," *WORLD News Group*, January 10, 2015.

30 See "Blasphemy in Pakistan: Bad-mouthing," *The Economist*, November 29, 2014.

carried out by Taliban forces at a Pakistani school.[31] Taliban forces are active in Afghanistan, too, with attacks targeting Christians for murder because of their faith.[32]

The situation in India is more complicated, with Muslim and Christian minorities at risk and sometimes suffering under the Hindu majority. Tensions between the three groups recently surfaced as the government considered a possible law against religious conversion.[33] Fortunately, Christians have been able to speak their mind on the issue,[34] but previous violence and the possibility of further persecution make the matter important and urgent.[35]

Eastern and Northeastern Asia

Finally, looking toward eastern and northeastern Asia, we have heard for years about the dynamic growth of unofficial but often evangelical Christian churches in parallel with and apart from the officially sanctioned churches of China. Growth comes with risks as the Communist government cracks down on the unofficial churches from time to time. Sometimes government officials move to tear down crosses or sometimes even raze sanctuaries, but this is only a recent chapter in decades of official persecution.[36] Physical persecution comes into play, too, with waves of arrests and detentions[37] and frequent attempts at intimidation. However, as far as we can tell from sketchy information that makes it out of China, the churches continue to grow and Christianity thrives. In China's neighbor, the Democratic Republic

31   See Qasim Nauman and Safdar Dawar, "Pakistan Schools Reopen After Peshawar Massacre in December," *The Wall Street Journal*, January 12, 2015.

32   See Mindy Belz, "Weekend attack targets Christians in Kabul," *WORLD News Group*, December 1, 2014.

33   See Shanoor Seervai, "The Arguments For and Against a National Anti-Conversion Law," *The Wall Street Journal*, January 9, 2015.

34   See Julia A. Seymour, "Christians demand Modi take a stand in India's conversion debate," *WORLD News Group*, January 12, 2015.

35   See Julia A. Seymour, "India's Christians protest after St. Sebastian's Church burns," *WORLD News Group*, December 8, 2014.

36   See Peter Berger, "Is the Chinese Regime Changing its Policy Toward Christianity?" *The American Interest*, June 11, 2014, and "China's Persecution of Christians May Make Them Stronger," *The American Interest*, July 28, 2014.

37   See June Cheng, "Chinese crackdown on churches continues with arrests, detentions," *WORLD News Group*, September 26, 2014.

of North Korea, the situation is much worse, with no churches allowed, with Christians sent to labor camps for re-education, and with rumors of death by torture. In a way, the situation in North Korea is reminiscent of emperor worship in times of the Roman Empire. The Communist government demands complete allegiance of the people and tolerates no rivals,[38] much less One who claims to be Lord of all.

General Observations

Looking across the area of the world where Christians see the worst of circumstances, we see brothers and sisters in the faith who are tenacious, faithful, loving, and often forgiving. They are sinners just like you and I, and they fail just like you and I. However, they also know our Lord and cherish His Word. He sustains them so that they can hang on, strengthens their faith under fire, and equips them to be loving and forgiving under amazing circumstances. And He uses them as witnesses to those who have eyes to see and ears to hear. What can we learn from them? How might they inspire us? How can we support them?

Christians and churches around the world experience more oppression and persecution than we can review in this book.[39] All we can do here is paint the picture with broad strokes to help establish why we need to know more, and why understanding is even more valuable than knowing. However, even our limited situation analysis leads us to several useful observations and suggestions.

First, even if the situation seems dire, particularly in Muslim and communist countries, our Lord is at work behind the scenes to rescue people from the darkness of sin. For example, rumors keep surfacing about Muslims, sometimes in large numbers, professing faith in Jesus Christ.[40] Conversion from Islam to Christianity is a capital offense in many Muslim countries, so these people are at risk of death if their new faith becomes known. Some

---

38 See the 2015 World Watch List: North Korea, Open Doors International (www.opendoorsusa.org/christian-persecution/world-watch-list/north-korea/).

39 See Morgan Lee, "Pope: More Persecuted Christians Today Than Ever Before," *The Christian Post*, July 1, 2014.

40 See Warren Cole Smith, "The rising tide of Muslim converts to Christianity," *WORLD News Group*, July 28, 2014; Mindy Belz, "Not Your Headline News," *WORLD News Group*, May 31, 2014.

of them make public confession, even preaching the Word, at great personal risk. Others stay below the radar and witness to God's grace privately as opportunities arise. The situation is somewhat similar in some of the communist countries, where public profession of the faith invites disaster if governing authorities take offense. These circumstances make it difficult to know how many conversions happen, how large of a faithful remnant of believers God has planted or preserved, or how the situation might evolve. It also makes it important to protect personal identities so that the authorities cannot easily find and attack Christians.

Sometimes questions arise, asking if the persecution is real, and how we know if people are oppressed because of their faith or just because they are sort of in the way, in the wrong place at the wrong time. For example, does the Islamic State or Boko Haram attack Christians because they are Christians or because they are attacking an area of a country and Christians (as well as those of other faiths) just happen to live there? The answer might be yes to one or yes to the other or yes to both, but on a practical level the answer may not matter. It is hard to know how to reply to those who ask if persecution is real when it is so easy to see its effects in deaths, suffering, and forced migrations. At least those asking academic questions seem to sense that something may be happening that is worth asking about, which suggests they may be on a path toward greater understanding.

It is useful to notice how God works with the remnant He preserves in places of hostility and persecution,[41] and how He works with refugees who flee those areas for other countries. He uses the remnant as a witness to those around, including their persecutors. And at least some of the non-Christians who flee civil wars, devastated economies, and oppression find new homes in other countries—countries with religious freedom. There they receive the Word, hear and believe, rejoice in new freedom in Christ, and sometimes even become evangelists!

We know that our brothers and sisters in Christ are under attack in many parts of the world, and they are part of the Body of Christ, just as we are part of the Body of Christ. If they suffer, we suffer. The fact is that God has dispersed or placed us where He wants us to serve as ambassadors of Christ. And all of this affects the sowing of God's Word, seed for salvation. The

---

41   See Mindy Belz, "Christmastime, still," *WORLD News Group*, December 19, 2014.

more we know about the oppression and persecution facing Christians in other parts of the world, the harder it is to turn a deaf ear or a blind eye to their plight. At the same time, the more we know about how God is moving in different parts of the

If they suffer, we suffer.

world,[42] the harder it is to not want to walk with Him in His work.

Taking this line of thinking a little further, what can we learn from the suffering of our brothers and sisters? How can we learn from their example? This is worth exploring because it helps us understand their situation a little better, helps us know more about how to support them, and prepares us for that time when we will encounter suffering (note that I say "when" and not "if"). We will ponder these questions later as we explore common and special options for responding to hostility, and as we ask what those options might look like when put into practice.

So how can we know more about what is happening to our fellow Christians in other parts of the U.S. or other parts of the world? Why don't we hear more about these topics in the news? Where can we go for more information? As mentioned before, many countries where Christians are persecuted try to keep that kind of information under wraps. One might think they were ashamed of it, but it could simply be that they don't want the word to get out because it might invite some kind of resistance or push-back from other countries or even from elements of their own population. Any relevant information that does make it out of the country can be difficult to verify, and its public disclosure might endanger Christians or their families who still remain in the country. Even then, the United States government and the news media often choose not to report on persecution of Christians—after all, such topics do not win a lot of votes or sell much airtime or newspapers! More seriously, public disclosure might undermine

---

42 In John 3:5–8, Jesus explains, "Truly, truly, I say to you, unless one is born of water and the Spirit, he cannot enter the kingdom of God. That which is born of the flesh is flesh, and that which is born of the Spirit is spirit. Do not marvel that I said to you, 'You must be born again.' The wind blows where it wishes, and you hear its sound, but you do not know where it comes from or where it goes. So it is with everyone who is born of the Spirit." For purposes of this discussion, we note that the Holy Spirit is active and working, bringing people to rebirth in faith, wherever He wills. First Corinthians 12:11 confirms this sovereign activity of the Spirit when it says, "All these [spiritual gifts in the Church] are empowered by one and the same Spirit, who apportions to each one individually as He wills."

political positions or desired political narratives, and if that happened it would tarnish the credibility of politicians or mainstream news media.

If you want to know more, you need to take the initiative to seek out reliable, astute news sources on the Internet or among the news media. Further, it's important to discern the worldview of each news organization you use so that you can understand how their belief system shows up in which stories they choose to ignore; which they choose to report; how accurately they report news; and to what extent their reporting, commentary, interpretations, and inadvertent distortions are trustworthy. For completeness, you may also want to periodically check a few international sources, because they will report events from a different view, and it enriches your understanding to have that additional perspective. They will also pick up on news stories that escape the notice of U.S. news organizations. Some very good news sources show up in the footnotes of this book, and you can find those and others online, on the air, or in print. Some of the organizations listed in Appendix 1 provide additional help by collecting, consolidating, and reporting hard-to-obtain information from sources that might normally be out of reach for you or for me.

⌘⌘

Discussion Questions

1. Do you believe that you have personally experienced Christian persecution? How so?

2. Have you seen any examples of hostility toward Christians in your community? If so, how did you feel about it, and what did you do?

3. How would you know if you were encountering hostility because of your faith, or if it was just an honest difference of opinion? How might this present an opportunity to share your faith?

4. As a Christian and church member, how much influence do you and your church have on values and decisions in the community around you? Why do you think this is so?

5. How do you think the situation in your area of the country is changing with respect to religious freedom? What about the nation as a whole?

2

Theological Understanding of Hostility

God's people have experienced hostility ever since the strife between Cain and Abel. We need to understand hostility from a biblical point of view to be able to distinguish reality from misperceptions, to avoid simply reacting to circumstances, and above all to help us clearly see things from God's perspective. We need wisdom and understanding to correctly discern the situation and our options to respond. However, we also need to proceed honestly and prudently.

If what we view as hostility comes in response to our own sinful behavior, we should not be quick to assign blame to others. For example, if we sin against our neighbor, we should not be surprised if he responds in kind. If we break the law, we should expect government punishment[1] and should not automatically label such punishment as hostility. Romans 13:1–4 explains,

---

1 Romans 13:1–4 makes clear that God expects government to punish lawbreakers, yet there are times when civil disobedience may be appropriate. See the Commission on Theology and Church Relations report *Civil Obedience and Disobedience* (St. Louis: The Lutheran Church—Missouri Synod, 1967) for further discussion of this topic.

Let every person be subject to the governing authorities. For there is no authority except from God, and those that exist have been instituted by God. Therefore whoever resists the authorities resists what God has appointed, and those who resist will incur judgment. For rulers are not a terror to good conduct, but to bad. Would you have no fear of the one who is in authority? Then do what is good, and you will receive his approval, for he is God's servant for your good. But if you do wrong, be afraid, for he does not bear the sword in vain. For he is the servant of God, an avenger who carries out God's wrath on the wrongdoer.

We must not discount the reality of hostility toward Christians and the Church, but we must first seek understanding and be honest about any role we might have played that created the situation.

Writing to Christians dispersed, or seeded, by God throughout the world, Peter's first letter provides a valuable framework and starting point for understanding our circumstances, hostility we might encounter, and options to respond. In 1 Peter 1:6–7, the apostle first explains that although Christians inevitably experience grief and trials at one time or another, these difficulties will not overcome our joy in what God has done for us through Jesus Christ:

In this you rejoice, though now for a little while, if necessary, you have been grieved by various trials, so that the tested genuineness of your faith—more precious than gold that perishes though it is tested by fire—may be found to result in praise and glory and honor at the revelation of Jesus Christ.

Grief and trials are only temporary, and they serve to test our faith. This testing, or proving, strengthens our character and provides a powerful witness to others.

Second, Peter indicates that while Christians may suffer unjustly, for the sake of righteousness, we will also be blessed:

Now who is there to harm you if you are zealous for what is good? But even if you should suffer for righteousness' sake, you will be blessed. Have no fear of them, nor be troubled, but in your hearts honor Christ the Lord as holy, always being prepared to make a defense to anyone who asks you for a reason for the hope that is in you; yet do it with gentleness and respect, having a good conscience, so that, when you are slandered, those who revile your good behavior in Christ may be put to shame. For it is better to suffer for doing good, if that should be God's will, than for doing evil. (1 Peter 3:13–17)

Therefore, rather than being anxious, whining, or grumbling, we should keep Christ in our hearts and be prepared to take advantage of opportunities to explain the hope and faith God gives us.

Finally, Peter's letter helps us keep our perspective through the turmoil. He wrote:

Beloved, do not be surprised at the fiery trial when it comes upon you to test you, as though something strange were happening to you. But rejoice insofar as you share Christ's sufferings, that you may also rejoice and be glad when His glory is revealed. If you are insulted for the name of Christ, you are blessed, because the Spirit of glory and of God rests upon you. But let none of you suffer as a murderer or a thief or an evildoer or as a meddler. Yet if anyone suffers as a Christian, let him not be ashamed, but let him glorify God in that name. For it is time for judgment to begin at the household of God; and if it begins with us, what will be the outcome for those who do not obey the gospel of God? And "If the righteous is scarcely saved, what will become of the ungodly and the sinner?" Therefore let those who suffer according to God's will entrust their souls to a faithful Creator while doing good. (1 Peter 4:12–19)

He appears to have had in mind Matthew 5:11–12, where Jesus taught in Peter's presence: "Blessed are you when others revile you and persecute you and utter all kinds of evil against you falsely on My account. Rejoice and be glad, for your reward is great in heaven, for so they persecuted the prophets who were before you." If Jesus, our Master, suffers, so also will we suffer as His followers. We will suffer, but we will be in the good company of God's prophets and of our Lord Himself as we remain assured of our hope of salvation! God provides assurance, uses trials to strengthen us, turns trials into opportunities to share the Gospel with others, and helps us keep things in His perspective.

Exhorting the Church in Corinth and (since the letter was meant to be shared with others) the Church at large, the apostle Paul comments on the enduring value of affliction and suffering in 2 Corinthians 1:3–11, writing:

> Blessed be the God and Father of our Lord Jesus Christ, the Father of mercies and God of all comfort, who comforts us in all our affliction, so that we may be able to comfort those who are in any affliction, with the comfort with which we ourselves are comforted by God. For as we share abundantly in Christ's sufferings, so through Christ we share abundantly in comfort too. If we are afflicted, it is for your comfort and salvation; and if we are comforted, it is for your comfort, which you experience when you patiently endure the same sufferings that we suffer. Our hope for you is unshaken, for we know that as you share in our sufferings, you will also share in our comfort. For we do not want you to be unaware, brothers, of the affliction we experienced in Asia. For we were so utterly burdened beyond our strength that we despaired of life itself. Indeed, we felt that we had received the sentence of death. But that was to make us rely not on ourselves but on God who raises the dead. He delivered us from such a deadly peril, and He will deliver us. On Him we have set our hope that He will deliver us again. You also must help us by prayer, so that many will give thanks on our behalf for the blessing granted us through the prayers of many.

First, the apostle points out that God comforts us in our affliction, and this in turn makes us able to comfort others in their affliction (v. 4). Then he states that we share in affliction so that we may share in God's comfort (v. 7), with the emphasis on the word *share* reflecting the value of affliction and comfort in strengthening our unity and fellowship in Christ. Next, he draws from his own experience, sharing that affliction caused him to rely upon God (v. 9) and helped him avoid the all-too-common snare of self-reliance. Finally, he points out that as we support each other in prayer, we have the privilege of seeing God at work in each other's lives, leading us to thank God for His blessing (v. 11). We do not seek suffering or affliction, but God uses it to equip us to comfort and support others, to strengthen our Christian fellowship, to teach us to rely on Him rather than ourselves, and to give us reason to thank Him in prayer. But from where does hostility arise to afflict Christians and cause their suffering? We will explore this question next.

Hostility because of Sin

Every person since Adam and Eve, except for Jesus, is a sinner. Sin is the main root of hostility toward God and His people. A fundamental attribute of sin is each person's desire for sovereignty and self-interest, which then strives against God's sovereignty and selfless interest. This began when Adam and Eve decided that they wanted God-like knowledge in order to "be like God," and then they disobeyed His express command:

> **Sin is the main root of hostility toward God and His people.**

Now the serpent was more crafty than any other beast of the field that the LORD God had made. He said to the woman, "Did God actually say, 'You shall not eat of any tree in the garden'?" And the woman said to the serpent, "We may eat of the fruit of the trees in the garden, but God said, 'You shall not eat of the fruit of the tree that is in the midst of the garden, neither shall you touch it, lest you die.'" But the serpent said to the woman, "You will not surely die. For God knows that when you eat of it your eyes will be opened, and you will be like God, knowing good and evil." So when the woman saw that the tree was good for food, and that it was a delight to the eyes, and that the tree was to be desired to make one wise, she took of its fruit and ate, and she also gave some to her husband who was with her, and he ate. Then the eyes of both were opened, and they knew that they were naked. And they sewed fig leaves together and made themselves loincloths. (Genesis 3:1–7)

This rebellion has contaminated the human race ever since:[2] all people

---

2   Romans 5:12–19 explains the significance of Adam's disobedience, saying, "Therefore, just as sin

sin and all people rebel simply because all people are sinners. Anyone rebelling against God will feel hostility toward Jesus, since He is Lord, and our ingrained original sin means that we each want to be our own Lord, in His place. Paul summarized this miserable situation and the only way of escape in Romans 7:21–25, saying,

> So I find it to be a law that when I want to do right, evil lies close at hand. For I delight in the law of God, in my inner being, but I see in my members another law waging war against the law of my mind and making me captive to the law of sin that dwells in my members. Wretched man that I am! Who will deliver me from this body of death? Thanks be to God through Jesus Christ our Lord! So then, I myself serve the law of God with my mind, but with my flesh I serve the law of sin.

Those who refuse the rescue offered by Christ remain trapped in their own sin, and particularly in their own original sin, preferring to retain their own sovereignty and be their own god. When their claim of sovereignty runs into God's claim of sovereignty, these people become hostile toward Jesus Christ, who came as God in human flesh. Hostility toward Christ easily translates into hostility toward Christians, who make up the Body of Christ, and toward the Church, the Bride of Christ. This in turn fuels oppression and persecution.

Sin also leads to spiritual blindness and a futile striving for self-worth, with the blindness often exacerbated by materialism, greed, idolatry, or other self-serving behaviors. The apostle Paul described this corrosive

---

came into the world through one man, and death through sin, and so death spread to all men because all sinned—for sin indeed was in the world before the law was given, but sin is not counted where there is no law. Yet death reigned from Adam to Moses, even over those whose sinning was not like the transgression of Adam, who was a type of the one who was to come. But the free gift is not like the trespass. For if many died through one man's trespass, much more have the grace of God and the free gift by the grace of that one man Jesus Christ abounded for many. And the free gift is not like the result of that one man's sin. For the judgment following one trespass brought condemnation, but the free gift following many trespasses brought justification. For if, because of one man's trespass, death reigned through that one man, much more will those who receive the abundance of grace and the free gift of righteousness reign in life through the one man Jesus Christ. Therefore, as one trespass led to condemnation for all men, so one act of righteousness leads to justification and life for all men. For as by the one man's disobedience the many were made sinners, so by the one man's obedience the many will be made righteous."

power of sin and its destructive effects in Romans 1:18–32, portraying in grim detail the death spiral in which so many people are trapped by their rebellion against God:

> For the wrath of God is revealed from heaven against all ungodliness and unrighteousness of men, who by their unrighteousness suppress the truth. For what can be known about God is plain to them, because God has shown it to them. For His invisible attributes, namely, His eternal power and divine nature, have been clearly perceived, ever since the creation of the world, in the things that have been made. So they are without excuse. For although they knew God, they did not honor Him as God or give thanks to Him, but they became futile in their thinking, and their foolish hearts were darkened. Claiming to be wise, they became fools, and exchanged the glory of the immortal God for images resembling mortal man and birds and animals and creeping things.

> Therefore God gave them up in the lusts of their hearts to impurity, to the dishonoring of their bodies among themselves, because they exchanged the truth about God for a lie and worshiped and served the creature rather than the Creator, who is blessed forever! Amen.

> For this reason God gave them up to dishonorable passions. For their women exchanged natural relations for those that are contrary to nature; and the men likewise gave up natural relations with women and were consumed with passion for one another, men committing shameless acts with men and receiving in themselves the due penalty for their error.

> And since they did not see fit to acknowledge God, God gave them up to a debased mind to do what ought not to be done. They were filled with all manner of unrighteousness, evil, covetousness, malice. They are full of envy, murder, strife, deceit, maliciousness. They are gossips, slanderers, haters of

God, insolent, haughty, boastful, inventors of evil, disobedient to parents, foolish, faithless, heartless, ruthless. Though they know God's righteous decree that those who practice such things deserve to die, they not only do them but give approval to those who practice them.

Since sin involves self-interest and self-sovereignty over and against the lordship of Christ, actions that seem logical from a personal (i.e., selfish, narrow, and sinful) point of view will often be at perverse odds with actions that are logical from God's (i.e., selfless, larger, and holy) point of view. This contrast shows up in how or where people seek personal validation and fulfillment and extends to how people respond to Christians or Christian ministry: for a simple example, expanding a Christian shelter for the homeless might be well received by those wishing to feed, shelter, and witness to the homeless in the name of God, but opposed by people with selfish interests who object to bringing "undesirables" into the neighborhood. More seriously, people with belief systems (i.e., religions) that require them to establish their own self-worth and righteousness will typically gravitate toward one of two reactions when they learn of God's grace in Jesus Christ: either they embrace it with joy and relief or they utterly reject it because it threatens their own sovereignty.[3] Directly or indirectly, this lust lies beneath much of the hostility and persecution directed toward Christians today.

Sin relates to our suffering or affliction in at least two other ways. First, we noted earlier that if we suffer punishment, we should examine ourselves to see if we have done wrong in God's eyes or in the eyes of the authorities He places over us. If we have done wrong in one of these ways, then we indulge in a self-serving deception if we try to rationalize punishment for our sin by claiming that it is persecution against us as Christians.

Sin can trip us up in a second way too. We know that we are to take up our cross and follow Christ, but this is to be a cross God gives us rather than one of our own making. We see this in Matthew 16:24–26, where, "Jesus told His disciples, 'If anyone would come after Me, let him deny himself and take

---

3   C. S. Lewis picked up on this lust for sovereignty and its implications and explored it in his book *The Great Divorce*. The book's plot involves meeting a series of characters who either embrace God's grace or reject it in favor of their own will, choosing to spend eternity away from God.

up his cross and follow Me. For whoever would save his life will lose it, but whoever loses his life for My sake will find it. For what will it profit a man if he gains the whole world and forfeits his soul? Or what shall a man give in return for his soul?'" We cannot save our own life or our own soul by any of our own efforts. So also any cross we bear worthily cannot come from our own contrivances. Sin can trick us when pride leads us to look for affliction rather than waiting for it to come to us. Looking for affliction smacks of self-will, and puts us at odds with God's will. Jesus set an example for us in this regard when He avoided arrest and prosecution rather than seeking it. John 7:3–8, for example, shows Jesus following His Father's will rather than His brother's advice:

> So His brothers said to Him, "Leave here and go to Judea, that Your disciples also may see the works You are doing. For no one works in secret if he seeks to be known openly. If You do these things, show Yourself to the world." For not even His brothers believed in Him. Jesus said to them, "My time has not yet come, but your time is always here. The world cannot hate you, but it hates Me because I testify about it that its works are evil. You go up to the feast. I am not going up to this feast, for My time has not yet fully come."

Once the right time (God's timing) arrived, though, He went to the Garden of Gethsemane and suffered the arrest that led to His trial and crucifixion:

> When Jesus had spoken these words, He went out with His disciples across the brook Kidron, where there was a garden, which He and His disciples entered. Now Judas, who betrayed Him, also knew the place, for Jesus often met there with His disciples. . . . So the band of soldiers and their captain and the officers of the Jews arrested Jesus and bound Him. (John 18:1–2, 12)

Opposition to Christ

Related to the first root, sin, we find the second root of hostility in the world's opposition to the person and lordship of Jesus Christ. Individual personal rebellions coalesce into rebellion by groups, communities, and entire peoples. Fundamentally, the world's hostility toward Christ goes hand in hand with a collective rebellion against God the Creator. Paul described how the world first accepts, then endorses, and finally encourages ungodly behavior, and how this spiral downward develops as God lets people have their own way in how they choose to live (see Romans 1:24, 26, and 28 in the context of Romans 1:18–32 on pp. 57–58). The world's rebellion against God also shows up when people are not willing to listen to God's truth. Rather than hearing God's Word, which implies recognition of God's authority, people seek out teachers who will tell them what they want to hear. Second Timothy 4:3–4 warns, "For the time is coming when people will not endure sound teaching, but having itching ears they will accumulate for themselves teachers to suit their own passions, and will turn away from listening to the truth and wander off into myths."

> **People seek out teachers who will tell them what they want to hear.**

When the Word became flesh, even Christ's own people rejected Him out of hand. As John 1:10–11 notes, "He was in the world, and the world was made through Him, yet the world did not know Him. He came to His own, and His own people did not receive Him." Later, Jesus warned His disciples that the world would hate them just as it already hated Him.[4] He explained that hatred would arise because He had chosen

---

4 Just before sending His disciples out for ministry without Him along to run interference, Jesus gave them marching orders in Matthew 10:16–23, saying,

Behold, I am sending you out as sheep in the midst of wolves, so be wise as serpents and innocent as doves. Beware of men, for they will deliver you over to courts and flog you in their synagogues, and you will be dragged before governors and kings for My sake, to bear witness before them and the Gentiles. When they deliver you over, do not be anxious how you are to speak or what you are to say, for what you are to say will be given to you in that hour. For it is not you who speak, but the Spirit of your Father speaking through you. Brother will deliver brother over to death, and the father his child, and children will rise against parents and have them put to death, and you will be hated by all for My name's sake. But the one who endures to the end will be saved. When they persecute you in one town, flee to the next, for truly, I say to you, you will not have gone through all the towns of Israel before the Son of Man comes.

them out of the world and because they were no longer of the world. In fact, the hatred derives from our belonging to Jesus. Indeed, we are tied to the identity of Christ in at least four ways besides the obvious fact that as Christians we bear His name.

1. We have been adopted into God's family. "But to all who did receive Him, who believed in His name, He gave the right to become children of God" (John 1:12).

2. Christians are brothers and sisters of Christ. "But He answered them, 'My mother and My brothers are those who hear the word of God and do it'" (Luke 8:21).

3. The Church is the Body of Christ on earth. "Now you are the body of Christ and individually members of it" (1 Corinthians 12:27).

4. The Church is the Bride of Christ. "Husbands, love your wives, as Christ loved the church and gave Himself up for her. . . . 'Therefore a man shall leave his father and mother and hold fast to his wife, and the two shall become one flesh.' This mystery is profound, and I am saying that it refers to Christ and the church" (Ephesians 5:25, 31–32).

With so many and such close linkages between us as individuals and as a Church with our Lord and Savior, Jesus Christ, it is no wonder that rebellion and hostility toward God would translate into hostility, resentment, oppression, and persecution toward Christians and the Church.

Then, shortly before His arrest and crucifixion, Jesus further warned His disciples what to expect in John 15:20–24, saying,

Remember the word that I said to you: "A servant is not greater than his master." If they persecuted Me, they will also persecute you. If they kept My word, they will also keep yours. But all these things they will do to you on account of My name, because they do not know Him who sent Me. If I had not come and spoken to them, they would not have been guilty of sin, but now they have no excuse for their sin. Whoever hates Me hates My Father also. If I had not done among them the works that no one else did, they would not be guilty of sin, but now they have seen and hated both Me and My Father.

This raises a thought-provoking question: are God's people ever fully accepted and embraced by the surrounding culture? The answer seems to be no, at least not in any permanent or long-term sense. The world may tolerate or sometimes even admire Christians, and we may have the good fortune to live at peace for a time. If so, then this is a blessing worth asking of God, although 1 Timothy 2:1–4 seems to imply that we should pray for peace not for our own comfort and prosperity, but so that people can hear the Gospel and be saved:

> First of all, then, I urge that supplications, prayers, interces-
> sions, and thanksgivings be made for all people, for kings and
> all who are in high positions, that we may lead a peaceful and
> quiet life, godly and dignified in every way. This is good, and
> it is pleasing in the sight of God our Savior, who desires all
> people to be saved and to come to the knowledge of the truth.

Nevertheless, the fact that we live as citizens of heaven while still citizens on earth creates a tension that can quickly lead to the hostility Jesus predicted. More significantly, when we recall the hostility Jesus encountered as our Savior and that He calls us to follow in His footsteps, any ambiguity about whether Christians are fully accepted disappears. As Peter admonished, we should not be surprised if we suffer, for our Lord suffered before us. Esteem in the community[5] can soon give way to jealousy[6] and rage.[7] So the Early Church enjoyed the favor of all sorts of people in Jerusalem, but the situation deteriorated quickly and Stephen's martyrdom followed.

Since Christians and the Church are so inextricably linked to Christ, it is no surprise that hostility toward Christ transfers so easily into persecution of His people. Hostility toward Christians and the Church amounts to persecution of Christ. Jesus validated this linkage when He confronted Saul on the road to Damascus. Saul had been persecuting Christians since the

---

5   Acts 5:12b–13 records, "They [the Christians] were all together in Solomon's Portico. None of the rest dared join them, but the people held them in high esteem."

6   Acts 5:17–18 relates, "But the high priest rose up, and all who were with him (that is, the party of the Sadducees), and filled with jealousy they arrested the apostles and put them in the public prison."

7   Acts 5:33b says, "They were enraged and wanted to kill them."

stoning of Stephen, arresting them and seeing to their imprisonment. On his way to Damascus to find more Christians to persecute, he was stopped on the way by our risen, glorified Lord. Jesus did not ask Saul why he was persecuting Christians or the Church; instead, He said, "Saul, Saul, why are you persecuting *Me*?" When Saul asked who He was, Jesus replied, "I am Jesus, whom you are persecuting" (Acts 9:4–5, emphasis added). Jesus did not mention Christians or the Church, but He did not need to. To his dismay, Saul now understood exactly whom he had been persecuting. He already knew the Old Testament Scriptures well, and the words of Stephen's defense were still ringing in his memory, but Jesus was the catalyst that made the pieces fall into place. And this is still true to this day: Jesus is the catalyst who cannot be ignored, and hostility toward Christians and the Church is actually hostility toward Jesus Christ.

Persecuted for the Faith

The Prison Epistles of Paul remind us of the persecution that Paul and many early Christians suffered for the Gospel. In many parts of the modern world, Christians continue to suffer for their faith. This is to be expected, but God furnishes strength and endurance, and we continue to pray for our brothers and sisters in the faith.

During the apostle Paul's missionary journeys, Jews in various places resisted the Gospel message. On occasion, this resistance became violent. (See Paul's list of hardships at 2 Corinthians 11:23–33.)

This smoldering Jewish resentment was fanned into flames when Paul returned to Jerusalem after his third missionary journey and appeared in the temple. There, a group of Asian Jews incited a riot by publicly accusing Paul of forsaking the Law of Moses and polluting the temple by bringing a Gentile into the area reserved exclusively for Jews. The charges were false, but even so, they aroused the anti-Christian element in Jerusalem. Paul would doubtless have been stoned to death on the spot had not the Roman garrison commander intervened and brought a detachment of soldiers to stem the fury of the mob (Acts 21:27–36).

When an attempt by the apostle to defend himself before his Jewish accusers resulted in another near riot, the commander detained Paul (Acts 22). Hoping to have the charges against the apostle clarified, he called an informal meeting of the Jewish Council (Sanhedrin), but that meeting also degenerated into a shouting match. Meanwhile, Paul assured humane treatment for himself by informing the commander that he was a Roman citizen. When a plot on Paul's life was discovered, the commander had Paul removed to the seat of the imperial government at Caesarea (Acts 23).

With his arrival at Caesarea, Paul began an almost five-year period of unjust and unwarranted captivity, hearings, and appeals. After several years of imprisonment in Caesarea, Paul was convinced that he would never receive a fair trial in either Jerusalem or Caesarea. So he exercised his right as a Roman citizen to appeal his case directly to the emperor in Rome. Festus, the Roman governor in Palestine at that time, somewhat unwillingly granted Paul his appeal. Acts 27–28 describe Paul's long and perilous journey to Rome.

At Rome, the appeal process dragged on for more than two years. During this time, though constantly chained to a guard, Paul was able to receive friends and continue his ministry.

We do not know why Paul's hearing was delayed so long in Rome. In his Epistle to the Philippians, which is considered the last of the four Prison Epistles—the others being Ephesians, Colossians, and Philemon—Paul informed the Philippians that his first hearing had taken place and that it had gone well. Though he did not foolishly ignore the possibility that the emperor might still rule against him, Paul was optimistic that he would be acquitted and set free.

Based on what Paul says in Philippians and the Pastoral Epistles, he was likely set free from this first Roman imprisonment (AD 58–60) and continued to work until he was imprisoned again in the general persecution of Christians that took place under Emperor Nero in AD 67. During this second imprisonment, Paul wrote 2 Timothy, the last testimony of a Christian man facing his earthly end.

—From *The Lutheran Study Bible* (St. Louis: Concordia, 2009), p. 2042

Spiritual Warfare

The third major root of hostility toward Christians involves spiritual warfare waged by the evil one against Jesus and His Church. Ephesians 6:12 describes it this way, "For we do not wrestle against flesh and blood, but against the rulers, against the authorities, against the cosmic powers over this present darkness, against the spiritual forces of evil in the heavenly places."

It is not obvious unless we look for it, but we can find evidence that spiritual warfare predates the Church. In addition to the evil one's deception of Adam and Eve, two glimpses of Satan attacking God's people show up in the Old Testament, long before Christ established His Church on earth. In 1 Chronicles 21:1, we see a short, revealing statement: "Then Satan stood against Israel and incited David to number Israel." In the second, more explicit case, Job 1:6–12 relates,

Now there was a day when the sons of God came to present themselves before the LORD, and Satan also came among them. The LORD said to Satan, "From where have you come?" Satan answered the LORD and said, "From going to and fro on the earth, and from walking up and down on it." And the LORD said to Satan, "Have you considered My servant Job, that there is none like him on the earth, a blameless and upright man, who

65

fears God and turns away from evil?" Then Satan answered the Lord and said, "Does Job fear God for no reason? Have You not put a hedge around him and his house and all that he has, on every side? You have blessed the work of his hands, and his possessions have increased in the land. But stretch out Your hand and touch all that he has, and he will curse You to Your face." And the Lord said to Satan, "Behold, all that he has is in your hand. Only against him do not stretch out your hand." So Satan went out from the presence of the Lord.

Job 2:1–7 follows up with,

Again there was a day when the sons of God came to present themselves before the Lord, and Satan also came among them to present himself before the Lord. And the Lord said to Satan, "From where have you come?" Satan answered the Lord and said, "From going to and fro on the earth, and from walking up and down on it." And the Lord said to Satan, "Have you considered my servant Job, that there is none like him on the earth, a blameless and upright man, who fears God and turns away from evil? He still holds fast his integrity, although you incited Me against him to destroy him without reason." Then Satan answered the Lord and said, "Skin for skin! All that a man has he will give for his life. But stretch out Your hand and touch his bone and his flesh, and he will curse You to Your face." And the Lord said to Satan, "Behold, he is in your hand; only spare his life." So Satan went out from the presence of the Lord and struck Job with loathsome sores from the sole of his foot to the crown of his head.

Job was devastated by the attacks he received from Satan. Since he could not know what was happening out of sight in the conversations between Satan and God, he struggled to understand what was happening to him and why. Perhaps had he known of the conversations before each attack arrived, he still would have wondered why it was so. In the end, though, he realized his footing and comfort in the faith God had given him. Job 19:25–26 records a profound statement of Job's faith in God's redemption and even includes an allusion to the bodily resurrection: "For I know that my Redeemer lives, and at the last He will stand upon the earth. And after my skin has been thus destroyed, yet in my flesh I shall see God." We have the same assurances from God as Job, and a lot more information available to us in the Bible, but we are not spared the possibility of spiritual attack. Many aspects of spiritual warfare are beyond our ability to see or comprehend, but this does not make spiritual warfare any less real or potent.[8]

Peter and Paul also each encountered a personal taste of Satan's attacks. Satan requested and received permission to sift Peter like wheat. Luke 22:31–32 records Jesus saying to Peter, "Simon, Simon, behold, Satan demanded to have you, that he might sift you like wheat, but I have prayed for you that your faith may not fail. And when you have turned again, strengthen your brothers." Jesus assured Peter that He had already prayed for him and implicitly promised that Peter would survive and later minister to the brothers, but He did not promise that Peter would understand all that the sifting entailed, either before, during, or after the spiritual attack. Neither did Jesus explain Satan's demands.

Paul received a thorn in the flesh from Satan, which simply could not have happened without God's permission, since God is sovereign and Satan is not. Second Corinthians 12:7–10 says,

> So to keep me from becoming conceited because of the surpassing greatness of the revelations, a thorn was given me in the flesh, a messenger of Satan to harass me, to keep me from becoming conceited. Three times I pleaded with the Lord about this, that it should leave me. But He said to me, "My grace is sufficient for you, for My power is made perfect in weakness." Therefore I will boast all the more gladly of my weaknesses, so that the power of Christ may rest upon me. For the sake of Christ, then, I am content with weaknesses, insults, hardships, persecutions, and calamities. For when I am weak, then I am strong.

---

8   See the article entitled "Divine Warfare" on pp. 71–73 for a broader discussion of warfare in general.

Even though Paul pleaded with the Lord for relief, he was directed to depend on God's grace. God enabled Paul to live for the glory of Christ in spite of his thorn, and this gives us hope that He will enable us to live for His glory through our own challenges.

> **He will enable us to live for His glory through our own challenges.**

The devil is no respecter of persons. He also attacked Jesus directly, challenging His identity and tempting Him in the wilderness immediately after His Baptism. Luke 4:1–13 provides an account of this conflict:

> And Jesus, full of the Holy Spirit, returned from the Jordan and was led by the Spirit in the wilderness for forty days, being tempted by the devil. And He ate nothing during those days. And when they were ended, He was hungry. The devil said to Him, "If you are the Son of God, command this stone to become bread." And Jesus answered him, "It is written, 'Man shall not live by bread alone.'" And the devil took Him up and showed Him all the kingdoms of the world in a moment of time, and said to Him, "To You I will give all this authority and their glory, for it has been delivered to me, and I give it to whom I will. If You, then, will worship me, it will all be Yours." And Jesus answered him, "It is written, 'You shall worship the Lord your God, and Him only shall you serve.'"

> And he took Him to Jerusalem and set Him on the pinnacle of the temple and said to Him, "If You are the Son of God, throw Yourself down from here, for it is written, 'He will command His angels concerning you, to guard you,' and 'On their hands they will bear you up, lest you strike your foot against a stone.'"

> And Jesus answered Him, "It is said, 'You shall not put the Lord your God to the test.'" And when the devil had ended every temptation, he departed from Him until an opportune time.

Jesus successfully resisted the challenges and temptations, but verse 13 tells us that immediately after this, the devil left Him "until an opportune time." In other words, the attacks were not over, as evil spirits later attempted to derail Jesus' ministry by shouting out His identity, Satan attacked Peter as described above, and the devil drove Judas to betray Jesus in the Garden of Gethsemane.

Recalling our identity in Christ, it should come as no surprise that we experience attacks from the evil one. First Peter 5:8–9 warns, "Be sober-minded; be watchful. Your adversary the devil prowls around like a roaring lion, seeking someone to devour. Resist him, firm in your faith, knowing that the same kinds of suffering are being experienced by your brotherhood throughout the world." Attacks from the evil one or his agents come in many forms, but his favorite tactics seem to include

- trying to break us away from the rest of the Body of Christ;

- isolating us from God's Word;

- immobilizing us with discouragement;

- dividing our fellowship;

- challenging the authority of God's Word; or

- challenging God's authority or integrity.

In John 8:44, Jesus tells us of Satan, "He was a murderer from the beginning, and does not stand in the truth, because there is no truth in him. When he lies, he speaks out of his own character, for he is a liar and the father of lies." Thus, his attacks may be direct and blatant, or they may be subtle and stealthy. Regardless of the form of attack, the evil one is an opportunist and may choose to provoke opposition or persecution whenever suitable openings arise.

Stepping back to take a broader view, we see that God brought an orderly creation out of nothing. A contemplative read of the first chapter of Genesis gives us a sense of godly order, but we can see the gist of it in Genesis 1:1–2 and 1:31a: "In the beginning, God created the heavens and the earth. The earth was without form and void, and darkness was over the face of the deep. And the Spirit of God was hovering over the face of the waters. . . . And God saw everything that He had made, and behold, it was very good." God also prefers order and peace to confusion when it comes to worship and spiritual practice. As 1 Corinthians 14:33 points out, "God is not a God of confusion but of peace." Actually, God is the only source of true peace, as recognized in every one of Paul's letters to the churches. (They each include a statement of prayer asking God to bless the Church with God's strong peace.)

In contrast, the sometimes seemingly random and yet intense attacks experienced today by Christians and the Church worldwide create turmoil and try to destroy our peace. At least some of these attacks reflect a mostly hidden warfare by spiritual forces of evil against the kingdom of God. The devil takes personal interest in such attacks, as we saw in 1 Peter 5:8–9, and we must not discount their reality or their power. Romans 5:3–5 tells us, "We rejoice in our sufferings, knowing that suffering produces endurance, and endurance produces character, and character produces hope, and hope does not put us to shame, because God's love has been poured into our hearts through the Holy Spirit who has been given to us." We might not realize it at the time, but God uses these experiences to shape or hone us into instruments for His ministry of redemption. Sometimes their net effect is simply to turn us toward our heavenly Father, much as a child might instinctively turn toward his father for protection. And sometimes, like Peter or even like Job, we are not able to understand the situation, its origin, or how or when God might use it. This makes it all the more vital to live by the faith God gives us. Our Lord is Commander in Chief, and He places us on the battlefield as part of a larger strategy to accomplish His plans.

Divine Warfare

Satan and Man's Sin Started Warfare

Before the rebellion of Satan, war did not exist. . . . Humanity's conflict is first vertical, because reprobate man naturally hates the just and holy God, and then horizontal, between people, even between husband and wife (Gen 3:16), who are united as one flesh.

The first point that must be made, then, is that wars will continue to flare up between sinful human beings as long as they live in this fallen world, in which Satan is at work. The devil is the original murderer, and he continues to foster hatred and killing. Christ himself declared that there would continue to be wars and rumors of war, and that "it is necessary for this to happen" (Mt 24:6; similar are Mk 13:7; Lk 21:9). Only when he returns in glory to bring this world to its end and fully subjugate Satan will war cease.

Therefore every utopian religion or philosophy that has the goal of eliminating all earthly warfare is doomed to fail because it fails to reckon with the total depravity of human nature and the ongoing activity of Satan in this world.

⌘⌘

Christ's Divine Warfare Achieves Victory and Salvation

The second and crucial point is that divine warfare is God's means for saving his chosen people. For the sake of OT Israel, God engaged in temporal and national warfare, while for the salvation of all believers of both Testaments, God won the spiritual war through the physical death of Jesus on the cross and his bodily resurrection. Without this divine warfare, mankind would have been doomed to eternity in hell, but God's warfare enabled Israel to inherit the promised land, and his victory on the cross has made all believers heirs of eternal life in the new heavens and new earth. . . .

The book of Joshua has striking historical records of the personal involvement of the Lord in the battles of Israel for the promised land. God told Israel that it was "not by [their] sword and not by [their] bow" that they were victorious over the Canaanites (Josh 24:12). The Lord himself must fight and achieve the victory for the benefit of his people, in keeping with the biblical doctrine of divine monergism (versus synergism) in salvation. . . .

⌘⌘

71

Divine Warfare as God's Just Punishment on Human Sin

A third point is that justified warfare is God's means to punish evildoers and that such punishment is necessary to curb sin and maintain temporal order. God carries out such punishment not only for the good and stability of societies, but also so that his church can do its proper work of proclaiming the Gospel. A pacifist religion or philosophy actually contributes to violence and iniquity by failing to curtail evildoers—by death if necessary. God may be patient for long periods of time, justice may be delayed, and evildoers may evade their temporal due, but the final day of reckoning will come.

To comprehend the twofold meaning of the military conquest of Canaan by Israel in the book of Joshua, we need to bear in mind that the Lord is a God of Law and Gospel, judgment and salvation. He damns the impenitent to eternity in hell and justifies penitent believers, making them heirs of eternal life in the new heavens and new earth. Both of these actions are expressions of his character as the one holy and righteous God. . . .

⌘⌘

The Church's Warfare Is Spiritual

We see the long history of divine warfare culminate at the cross in the suffering and death of Jesus Christ, who atoned vicariously for the sin and rebellion of the whole world. As he lay dead in the tomb, he appeared vanquished by the devil, who had entered his betrayer, Judas. But on earth's gladdest day, he rose as the victor, having conquered sin, Satan, and death. Paradoxically, the instrument of his death was his instrument of conquest: "Having disarmed the powers and authorities, he made a public spectacle of them, triumphing over them by the cross" (Col 2:15). He is the stronger man who has disarmed the strong man—the devil—and plundered the devil's palace (Lk 11:22) by freeing those the devil had kept in bondage. . . .

Through the preaching of the Gospel and administration of the Sacraments, lost sinners are transferred from the kingdom of Satan into the kingdom of God. This transfer took place through OT Israel too, as in the cases of the former prostitute Rahab and her family (Josh 6:22–25) and the Gibeonites (Joshua 9), who were spared, incorporated into God's Israel, and justified before God (Heb 11:31 and James 2:25 affirm this about Rahab). The Gibeonites even became sanctuary servants, cutting wood and drawing water for "the house of my [Joshua's] God" and "for the altar of the Lord" (Josh 9:23, 27).

The Christian Gospel in Word and Sacrament rescues the perishing from eternal destruction and fortifies them to do battle against the forces of evil within (the sinful flesh) and without (the devil and the world) that assail them. It is necessary for Christians to oppose detestable practices such as idolatry, sexual immorality, homosexuality, abortion, euthanasia, and occult practices, which correspond to the ancient abominations of the Canaanites. The church rightly prohibits God's people from engaging in such practices. The church also rightly endeavors to persuade society at large to prohibit such evils, and to do so Christians work peacefully through lawful means, not by violence. . . .

⌘⌘

A Christian View of Warfare Must Distinguish Law from Gospel

The church and individual Christians must carefully distinguish Law and Gospel in order to follow and implement what God's Word says about warfare. Physical warfare may be a justified use of force according to God's Law, since God uses nations, armies, and society's laws to punish evil and protect the common welfare. However, earthly warfare cannot bring about God's kingdom of grace, which comes only through the Gospel in Word and Sacrament. In the OT too, it was not Israel's warfare, but faith in God's acts of salvation in fulfillment of his Word that caused Rahab and the Gibeonites to be saved.

—From Adolph L. Harstad, *Joshua*, Concordia Commentary (St. Louis: Concordia, 2004), 256–66.

Before moving on to look at case studies from Scripture, we should note that any of these three roots of hostility (sin, opposition to Christ, and spiritual warfare) could lead to hostility and persecution in ways that we might not be able to explain. The roots are there, but like tree roots, we might not be able to see them even though they support and nourish things that we *can* see. Hostility and persecution are with us, regardless, so we must stay vigilant, standing our ground and fitted for spiritual battle with the armor of God.

Examples from Scripture

Events recorded in the Old and New Testaments illustrate a wide variety of instances in which hostility arose toward God's people and portray how they responded, sometimes for good and sometimes not. In many cases, we can infer, or sometimes Scripture tells us directly, how His people felt about their situation. Uniformly, these case histories point us to God's sovereignty over events His people experienced and illustrate His gifts of faith and, at times, deliverance. Frequently, these events provided a witness to God's power, grace, judgment, or mercy for God's people and for third party bystanders (individuals, families, and entire nations) who witnessed the events as they occurred.

Let us step back and look at a few selected occasions when God's people in the Old or New Testament experienced hostility. These accounts help show whether our circumstances are really new and help us understand what is happening when we experience hostility. Biblical case histories of God's people facing hostility can provide lessons about different kinds of situations. They can show how God might use such circumstances and, when He chooses, turn them around. The Bible contains plenty of material for review, so we will choose a few examples from various experiences of people of faith to highlight different aspects of hostility and its effects.

Abraham—Afraid of Others

> Abraham said, "I did it because I thought, 'There is no fear of God at all in this place, and they will kill me because of my wife.'" (Genesis 20:11)

> Then God said to him [Abimelech] in the dream, ". . . return the man's wife, for he is a prophet, so that he will pray for you, and you shall live. But if you do not return her, know that you shall surely die, you and all who are yours." (Genesis 20:6–7)

Do we ever experience fear of neighbors and community, and what they might do to us? Abraham, chosen by God and noted as a hero of the faith in Hebrews 11,[9] sometimes lived in fear of his neighbors and the governing

---

9   Hebrews 11:8–12, 17–19: "By faith Abraham obeyed when he was called to go out to a place that

authorities. On two separate occasions he hid the fact that Sarah was his wife, apparently thinking she would be taken by force because of her beauty and that he would lose his life in the process. Was it a matter of selfishness, pride, or something else that caused him to hide the truth? Regardless, since Abraham passed Sarah off as his sister, she was indeed taken from him both times,[10] at least temporarily, leaving him apparently helpless in his loss. Real or perceived behavior of Abraham's neighbors probably stoked his fears and raised doubts in his mind, and to some extent his fears were realized. Perhaps the limits of his faith led Abraham to believe that since neither Pharaoh nor the king of Gerar knew his God, they had no reason to fear God or His intervention. However, God is a lot bigger than a local deity, so this thinking might have reflected Abraham's limited understanding of the God who had called him to leave Ur and migrate to a new land. Providentially, in both cases, God intervened to protect Sarah and restore her to her husband. In the process, God relieved Abraham's fears, reminded him of His care, and taught first Pharaoh and then Abimelech something of His power and sovereignty.

Elijah—Isolated and Alone

[The LORD] said to him, "What are you doing here, Elijah?" He said, "I have been very jealous for the LORD, the God of hosts. For the people of Israel have forsaken Your covenant, thrown down Your altars, and killed Your prophets with the sword, and I, even I only, am left, and they seek my life, to take it away." (1 Kings 19:9b–10)

---

he was to receive as an inheritance. And he went out, not knowing where he was going. By faith he went to live in the land of promise, as in a foreign land, living in tents with Isaac and Jacob, heirs with him of the same promise. For he was looking forward to the city that has foundations, whose designer and builder is God. By faith Sarah herself received power to conceive, even when she was past the age, since she considered Him faithful who had promised. Therefore from one man, and him as good as dead, were born descendants as many as the stars of heaven and as many as the innumerable grains of sand by the seashore. . . . By faith Abraham, when he was tested, offered up Isaac, and he who had received the promises was in the act of offering up his only son, of whom it was said, 'Through Isaac shall your offspring be named.' He considered that God was able even to raise him from the dead, from which, figuratively speaking, he did receive him back.'" However, there is no mention of Abraham fearing for his life because the king wanted his wife.

10 Genesis 12:14–20 shows Abraham deferring to Pharaoh, in Egypt, and Genesis 20 relates a similar, somewhat later incident involving Abimelech, king of Gerar.

> The Lord said to him, "Go, return on your way to the wilderness of Damascus. And when you arrive, you shall anoint Hazael to be king over Syria. And Jehu the son of Nimshi you shall anoint to be king over Israel, and Elisha the son of Shaphat of Abel-meholah you shall anoint to be prophet in your place. . . . Yet I will leave seven thousand in Israel, all the knees that have not bowed to Baal, and every mouth that has not kissed him." (1 Kings 19:15–16, 18)

Sometimes we may feel isolated and alone, perhaps even feeling as though we are the last of God's people facing hostility and threats of violence. Elijah felt this way after his conflict with Ahaz, Jezebel, and the prophets of Baal.[11] In spiritual battle, he defeated the prophets of Baal at Mount Carmel and then, at God's instruction, prayed for the end of a three-year drought and (perhaps most important) that God would turn the hearts of Israel back to Him. Rain came almost immediately, marking Elijah's triumph in the name of God. However, when he and Ahab arrived in the capital city of Jezreel, Queen Jezebel cursed him and threatened his execution. Elijah's sense of victory turned to despair, and he fled for his life. Arriving at Mount Horeb (Mount Sinai, where God had met with Moses and given Israel the Ten Commandments during the exodus), he hid in a cave. His sense of defeat, feelings of being alone, and the hazardous situation after the triumph at Mount Carmel were all very real, yet God did not immediately soothe his feelings or remove the threats. Instead, He graciously provided Elijah with food and water; demonstrated His power and majesty by a theophany of wind, earthquake, and fire; assured him that he was not alone (God was with him, and there were still seven thousand people in Israel who did not worship Baal); and put him to work with new tasks that would further God's plans for Israel and His chosen people. In faith, rested and restored, Elijah left the cave and went about God's work.

---

11   First Kings 18:20–19:18 describes Elijah's encounter with Ahaz and Baal's prophets on Mount Carmel, followed by Jezebel's threats against his life, and his escape to Mount Horeb.

Daniel—Exiled into Political Persecution

> Then these men said, "We shall not find any ground for complaint against this Daniel unless we find it in connection with the law of his God." (Daniel 6:5)

> When Daniel knew that the document had been signed, he went to his house where he had windows in his upper chamber open toward Jerusalem. He got down on his knees three times a day and prayed and gave thanks before his God, as he had done previously. (Daniel 6:10)

In some situations, governing organizations or others in authority may threaten us with sanctions, penalties, or worse for practicing our faith. During the Babylonian exile, Daniel rose to one of the top three positions in the kingdom of Babylon's government, but he had enemies who decided the only way they could attack Daniel would be on the basis of his faith. Therefore, they conspired to pass a law forbidding him from praying to God. Daniel 6:5–10 relates,

> Then these men said, "We shall not find any ground for complaint against this Daniel unless we find it in connection with the law of his God." Then these high officials and satraps came by agreement to the king and said to him, "O King Darius, live forever! All the high officials of the kingdom, the prefects and the satraps, the counselors and the governors are agreed that the king should establish an ordinance and enforce an injunction, that whoever makes petition to any god or man for thirty days, except to you, O king, shall be cast into the den of lions. Now, O king, establish the injunction and sign the document, so that it cannot be changed, according to the law of the Medes and the Persians, which cannot be revoked." Therefore King Darius signed the document and injunction. When Daniel knew that the document had been signed, he went to his house where he had windows in his upper chamber open toward Jerusalem. He got down on his knees three times a day and prayed and gave thanks before his God, as he had done previously.

This was not just a matter of personal rivalry and office politics; it marked a competition between two different belief systems. Daniel knew that he would face capital punishment if he disobeyed, and he no doubt experienced genuine fear because of the hostility he faced. Regardless, when he knew the law had been enacted, he deliberately chose to continue his regular prayers, and he prayed where he knew others could see him. His enemies arrived at a time when they could find him praying, confronted him, and had him brought before the king for trial. Although he knew Daniel did not deserve death, under the law of the land the king had to place Daniel in a den of lions as a gruesome form of execution. Daniel knew in faith that God would care for him, but had no way to know in advance if God would spare him from the lions or if he would die that night and go to dwell in the house of the Lord. As David had described centuries earlier in Psalm 23:4a, 6b, "Even though I walk through the valley of the shadow of death, I will fear no evil, . . . and I shall dwell in the house of the LORD forever." God chose to spare Daniel from the lions, making Daniel's decision to put God above the law prohibiting his prayers an endorsement and witness to those around.

Shadrach, Meshach, and Abednego—Trial by Fire

> You are to fall down and worship the golden image that King Nebuchadnezzar has set up. And whoever does not fall down and worship shall immediately be cast into a burning fiery furnace. (Daniel 3:5b–6)

> Shadrach, Meshach, and Abednego answered and said to the king, "O Nebuchadnezzar, we have no need to answer you in this matter. If this be so, our God whom we serve is able to deliver us from the burning fiery furnace, and He will deliver us out of your hand, O king. But if not, be it known to you, O king, that we will not serve your gods or worship the golden image that you have set up." (Daniel 3:16–18)

At a different time during the Babylonian exile, Shadrach, Meshach, and Abednego (three of Daniel's friends) were ordered to worship an idolatrous image instead of God. Daniel 3:8–27 relates what happened:

Certain Chaldeans came forward and maliciously accused the Jews. They declared to King Nebuchadnezzar, ". . . There are certain Jews whom you have appointed over the affairs of the province of Babylon: Shadrach, Meshach, and Abednego. These men, O king, pay no attention to you; they do not serve your gods or worship the golden image that you have set up."

Then Nebuchadnezzar in furious rage commanded that Shadrach, Meshach, and Abednego be brought. So they brought these men before the king. Nebuchadnezzar answered and said to them, "Is it true, O Shadrach, Meshach, and Abednego, that you do not serve my gods or worship the golden image that I have set up? . . . If you do not worship, you shall immediately be cast into a burning fiery furnace. And who is the god who will deliver you out of my hands?"

Shadrach, Meshach, and Abednego answered and said to the king, "O Nebuchadnezzar, we have no need to answer you in this matter. If this be so, our God whom we serve is able to deliver us from the burning fiery furnace, and He will deliver us out of your hand, O king. But if not, be it known to you, O king, that we will not serve your gods or worship the golden image that you have set up."

Then Nebuchadnezzar . . . ordered the furnace heated seven times more than it was usually heated. . . . . Then these men were bound in their cloaks, their tunics, their hats, and their other garments, and they were thrown into the burning fiery furnace. . . .

Then King Nebuchadnezzar was astonished and rose up in haste. He declared to his counselors, "Did we not cast three men bound into the fire?" They answered and said to the king, "True, O king." He answered and said, "But I see four men unbound, walking in the midst of the fire, and they are not hurt; and the appearance of the fourth is like a son of the gods."

Then Nebuchadnezzar came near to the door of the burning fiery furnace; he declared, "Shadrach, Meshach, and Abednego, servants of the Most High God, come out, and come here!" Then Shadrach, Meshach, and Abednego came out from the fire. And the satraps, the prefects, the governors, and the king's counselors gathered together and saw that the fire had not had any power over the bodies of those men. The hair of their heads was not singed, their cloaks were not harmed, and no smell of fire had come upon them.

Shadrach, Meshach, and Abednego faced capital punishment if they refused to submit to the law, which had been enacted as part of a scheme to impose a uniform, pagan style of worship on the nation. They no doubt felt genuine fear because of the hostility they experienced, but they willingly faced death rather than compromise their faith. When the time came to worship the idol and they refused, they were arrested, bound, and thrown into a blast furnace. However, when the king looked into the furnace to see their fate, he could see them alive and apparently unharmed by the flames. Even more unexpectedly, the king could see a fourth person in the fire; this might have been an angel God sent to protect them. As in Daniel's case, although God saved the three men from a fiery death, this outcome was not guaranteed in advance. In fact, when on trial before the king for refusing to worship the idol, Shadrach, Meshach, and Abednego specifically acknowledged the possibility that God would let them suffer physical death and stated that they would rather die than obey the king's law by worshiping anyone but the living God. In effect, they told the king that they were in God's hands and would trust Him for the outcome—a strong witness in a dark situation!

Ezra and Nehemiah—Hostility at Work

I told them of the hand of my God that had been upon me for good, and also of the words that the king had spoken to me. And they said, "Let us rise up and build." So they strengthened their hands for the good work. But when Sanballat the Horonite and Tobiah the Ammonite servant and Geshem the Arab heard of it, they jeered at us and despised us and said,

"What is this thing that you are doing? Are you rebelling against the king?" Then I replied to them, "The God of heaven will make us prosper, and we His servants will arise and build, but you have no portion or right or claim in Jerusalem." (Nehemiah 2:18–20)

Ezra and Nehemiah encountered a different kind of opposition when they returned from Babylon to resettle Jerusalem after the exile. Both were men of faith, both had a vision for what God would like to see accomplished, and both led a substantial number of men and families to help them in their respective building programs. Ezra, a priest, was called to rebuild the temple, while Nehemiah was more of a manager and aimed to restore the city wall. The opposition they encountered reflected a subtle expansion from hostility toward a person's spiritual identity to include hostility toward their work and ministry.

Prominent citizens and officials of the region attempted to dissuade Ezra and his colleagues from their work upon their return to Jerusalem. It is unclear whether this was prompted by jealousy of God's people, since the local people believed they had inherited the land when God punished Jerusalem and sent them into exile several decades earlier, or if the opposition was driven by ego or economic motives, or if it was a combination of factors. Intimidation failed to stop the work, and the Jews would not let them claim a role in the rebuilding, fearing that either course of action would eventually take the work in a direction different from what God had in mind. When the local official's multicultural approach did not work, they conspired to misrepresent and slander the Jews in an attempt to invoke the king's authority to block it.

Ezra 4:4–6 describes the intimidation:

Then the people of the land discouraged the people of Judah and made them afraid to build and bribed counselors against them to frustrate their purpose, all the days of Cyrus king of Persia, even until the reign of Darius king of Persia. And in the reign of Ahasuerus, in the beginning of his reign, they wrote an accusation against the inhabitants of Judah and Jerusalem.

Ezra 5:2–5 describes what happened next:

> Zerubbabel the son of Shealtiel and Jeshua the son of Jozadak arose and began to rebuild the house of God that is in Jerusalem, and the prophets of God were with them, supporting them. At the same time Tattenai the governor of the province Beyond the River and Shethar-bozenai and their associates came to them and spoke to them thus: "Who gave you a decree to build this house and to finish this structure?" They also asked them this: "What are the names of the men who are building this building?" But the eye of their God was on the elders of the Jews, and they did not stop them until the report should reach Darius and then an answer be returned by letter concerning it.

Community leaders also tried to intimidate Nehemiah and his colleagues with repeated cycles of ridicule, bluster, and threats against their attempt to rebuild the city walls and gates. Nehemiah 2:17–19 describes the first cycle:

> Then I said to them, "You see the trouble we are in, how Jerusalem lies in ruins with its gates burned. Come, let us build the wall of Jerusalem, that we may no longer suffer derision." And I told them of the hand of my God that had been upon me for good, and also of the words that the king had spoken to me. And they said, "Let us rise up and build." So they strengthened their hands for the good work. But when Sanballat the Horonite and Tobiah the Ammonite servant and Geshem the Arab heard of it, they jeered at us and despised us and said, "What is this thing that you are doing? Are you rebelling against the king?"

A second cycle came in Nehemiah 4:1–3, which relates,

> Now when Sanballat heard that we were building the wall, he was angry and greatly enraged, and he jeered at the Jews. And he said in the presence of his brothers and of the army of Samaria, "What are these feeble Jews doing? Will they restore it for themselves? Will they sacrifice? Will they finish up in a

day? Will they revive the stones out of the heaps of rubbish, and burned ones at that?" Tobiah the Ammonite was beside him, and he said, "Yes, what they are building—if a fox goes up on it he will break down their stone wall!"

And Nehemiah 6:10–13 records yet a third cycle of opposition:

Now when I went into the house of Shemaiah the son of De-laiah, son of Mehetabel, who was confined to his home, he said, "Let us meet together in the house of God, within the temple. Let us close the doors of the temple, for they are coming to kill you. They are coming to kill you by night." But I said, "Should such a man as I run away? And what man such as I could go into the temple and live? I will not go in." And I understood and saw that God had not sent him, but he had pronounced the prophecy against me because Tobiah and Sanballat had hired him. For this purpose he was hired, that I should be afraid and act in this way and sin, and so they could give me a bad name in order to taunt me.

Such repeated opposition can have devastating effects on morale and minis-try, potentially immobilizing God's people in their work.

Ezra and Nehemiah responded with a clear-eyed understanding of the situation, collecting information at night and as needed to support their strategies, exhorting their colleagues to continue working in the name of the Lord, and posting guards and caching weapons in case they would need to repel an attack. They also rejected threats and bogus attempts to divert them from the work, and refused to negotiate their position. Each of them responded with a mix of prayer, theological understanding, political acumen, and practical management steps. In the end, Ezra and Nehemiah stayed the course and completed their work; their opponents were frustrated as God heard His people's prayers and brought them through their difficulties.

Jesus—Temptation, Opposition, and Violence

When they heard these things, all in the synagogue were filled with wrath. And they rose up and drove Him out of the town and brought Him to the brow of the hill on which their town was built, so that they could throw Him down the cliff. But passing through their midst, He went away. (Luke 4:28–30)

For this reason the Father loves Me, because I lay down My life that I may take it up again. No one takes it from Me, but I lay it down of My own accord. I have authority to lay it down, and I have authority to take it up again. This charge I have received from My Father. (John 10:17–18)

Our Savior ran into apathy, opposition, and hostility many times during His ministry. It is worth reading and studying the Gospels to see how Jesus diagnosed and dealt with each incident as it arose. The first opposition recorded in the Gospels (other than Herod's attempt to murder the baby Jesus) was the tempting and testing from Satan immediately after Jesus' Baptism. When Satan failed to trip up Jesus, he departed until a more opportune time (as we saw earlier in Luke 4:13). Later, the disciples ran into their own difficulties immediately after coming down the mountain after the transfiguration. Matthew 17:14–20a relates,

And when they came to the crowd, a man came up to Him and, kneeling before Him, said, "Lord, have mercy on my son, for he is an epileptic and he suffers terribly. For often he falls into the fire, and often into the water. And I brought him to Your disciples, and they could not heal him." And Jesus answered, "O faithless and twisted generation, how long am I to be with you? How long am I to bear with you? Bring him here to Me." And Jesus rebuked the demon, and it came out of him, and the boy was healed instantly. Then the disciples came to Jesus privately and said, "Why could we not cast it out?" He said to them, "Because of your little faith."

By analogy, we should not be surprised to encounter a rough time soon after a spiritual mountaintop experience.

The situation around Jesus was often volatile. The mood in His hometown of Nazareth, for example, shifted from favor to hostility in only minutes, and led to an attempt against His life. This is reported in Luke 4:22–30:

And all spoke well of Him and marveled at the gracious words that were coming from His mouth. And they said, "Is not this Joseph's son?" And He said to them, "Doubtless you will quote to Me this proverb, 'Physician, heal yourself.' What we have heard You did at Capernaum, do here in Your hometown as well." And He said, "Truly, I say to you, no prophet is acceptable in his hometown. But in truth, I tell you, there were many widows in Israel in the days of Elijah, when the heavens were shut up three years and six months, and a great famine came over all the land, and Elijah was sent to none of them but only to Zarephath, in the land of Sidon, to a woman who was a widow. And there were many lepers in Israel in the time of the prophet Elisha, and none of them was cleansed, but only Naaman the Syrian." When they heard these things, all in the synagogue were filled with wrath. And they rose up and drove Him out of the town and brought Him to the brow of the hill on which their town was built, so that they could throw Him down the cliff. But passing through their midst, He went away.

Later, Jesus encountered a Gentile community that, while not directly hostile, feared Him and asked Him to leave their area after He had healed a man with a demon. Luke 8:34–37 tells us what happened:

When the herdsmen saw what had happened, they fled and told it in the city and in the country. Then people went out to see what had happened, and they came to Jesus and found the man from whom the demons had gone, sitting at the feet of Jesus, clothed and in his right mind, and they were afraid. And those who had seen it told them how the demon-possessed man had been healed. Then all the people of the surrounding country of the Gerasenes asked Him to depart from them, for they were seized with great fear. So He got into the boat and returned.

Strange as it may seem, apparently the spiritual and moral authority of Jesus (and, by extension, Christians) can provoke fear in the hearts of onlookers.

How did Jesus stay on track with His Father's will, and how did He maintain poise and readiness for whatever the evil one, the world, or circumstances might throw at Him next? He spent considerable time in prayer, in private,[12] to keep His balance from one event to the next. We will discuss prayer and other helpful spiritual disciplines, and consider the role they play in our response to hostility and worse, in chapter 4.

Of course, Jesus encountered the most extreme forms of hostility coming from all directions in the course of His arrest, trial, and crucifixion. Hostility directed at Jesus extends to His disciples and to His Church, and it centers on our identity in Christ and our work of evangelism and teaching under the Great Commission. Jesus said as much to His disciples when He warned of hostility and persecution:

> Behold, I am sending you out as sheep in the midst of wolves, so be wise as serpents and innocent as doves. Beware of men, for they will deliver you over to courts and flog you in their synagogues, and you will be dragged before governors and kings for My sake, to bear witness before them and the Gentiles. When they deliver you over, do not be anxious how you are to speak or what you are to say, for what you are to say will be given to you in that hour. For it is not you who speak, but the Spirit of your Father speaking through you. Brother will deliver brother over to death, and the father his child, and children will rise against parents and have them put to death, and you will be hated by all for My name's sake. But the one who endures to the end will be saved. When they persecute you in one town, flee to the next, for truly, I say to you, you will not have gone through all the towns of Israel before the Son of Man comes. A disciple is not above his teacher, nor a servant above his master. It is enough for the disciple to be like his teacher, and the servant like his master. If they have called

---

12   Examples are found in Matthew 26:36, "Then Jesus went with them to a place called Gethsemane, and He said to His disciples, 'Sit here, while I go over there and pray'"; Mark 1:35, "And rising very early in the morning, while it was still dark, He departed and went out to a desolate place, and there He prayed"; and Luke 11:1, "Now Jesus was praying in a certain place, and when He finished, one of His disciples said to Him, 'Lord, teach us to pray, as John taught his disciples.'"

the master of the house Beelzebul, how much more will they malign those of his household. (Matthew 10:16–25)

Further, Jesus linked persecution of the Church with persecution of His own person when He met Saul on the road to Damascus:

Saul, still breathing threats and murder against the disciples of the Lord, went to the high priest and asked him for letters to the synagogues at Damascus, so that if he found any belonging to the Way, men or women, he might bring them bound to Jerusalem. Now as he went on his way, he approached Damascus, and suddenly a light from heaven shone around him. And falling to the ground he heard a voice saying to him, "Saul, Saul, why are you persecuting Me?" And he said, "Who are you, Lord?" And He said, "I am Jesus, whom you are persecuting." (Acts 9:1–5)

With our identity tied so closely to Jesus Christ, we should be surprised if we do not experience opposition in various forms, along with the sadness, pain, and other emotions that our Lord experienced. However, our experience will also include joy and relief because of the redemption, security, and hope of eternal life we have in Christ.

Peter and John—On Trial for the Gospel

And as they were speaking to the people, the priests and the captain of the temple and the Sadducees came upon them, greatly annoyed because they were teaching the people and proclaiming in Jesus the resurrection from the dead. And they arrested them and put them in custody until the next day, for it was already evening. (Acts 4:1–3)

So they called them and charged them not to speak or teach at all in the name of Jesus. But Peter and John answered them, "Whether it is right in the sight of God to listen to you rather than to God, you must judge, for we cannot but speak of what we have seen and heard." (Acts 4:18–20)

The Early Church felt the reality of Jesus' warning almost immediately. Shortly after Pentecost, the ruling religious council of Jerusalem called Peter and John to account for healing a crippled man. Alarmed by the Gospel, they arrested Peter and John, brought them to trial, ordered them to stop teaching in the name of Jesus, and attempted to stop the ministry with threats and intimidation (Acts 4:1–22).[13] With the full authority of the religious establishment opposing them, Peter and John defended themselves with unexpected boldness, apparently reflecting the truth of Jesus' promise (see Matthew 10:19–20 in our earlier discussion) that His disciples would be given words for such occasions. Although the Jewish authorities had singled out Peter and John, the rest of the narrative shows that the church leadership took this as a broad threat against the whole ministry. Once Peter and John reported back to them, rather than making plans to retreat or compromise God's work, they prayed for boldness and continued their ministry.[14]

Opposition to the Early Church also arose from the secular government. For example, Herod arrested and executed James the brother of John, instigated violence against other members of the church, and then arrested Peter and held him for trial. Acts 12:1–5 explains,

> About that time Herod the king laid violent hands on some who belonged to the church. He killed James the brother of John with the sword, and when he saw that it pleased the Jews,

---

13 Key verses in this passage include verses 1–2, "And as they were speaking to the people, the priests and the captain of the temple and the Sadducees came upon them, greatly annoyed because they were teaching the people and proclaiming in Jesus the resurrection from the dead"; verse 3, "And they arrested them and put them in custody"; verse 7, "And when they had set them in the midst, they inquired, 'By what power or by what name did you do this?'"; verses 17–18, "'But in order that it may spread no further among the people, let us warn them to speak no more to anyone in this name.' So they called them and charged them not to speak or teach at all in the name of Jesus"; and verse 21, "And when they had further threatened them, they let them go, finding no way to punish them, because of the people, for all were praising God for what had happened."

14 Acts 4:24–30 reports, "And when they heard it, they lifted their voices together to God and said, 'Sovereign Lord, who made the heaven and the earth and the sea and everything in them, who through the mouth of our father David, Your servant, said by the Holy Spirit, 'Why did the Gentiles rage, and the peoples plot in vain? The kings of the earth set themselves, and the rulers were gathered together, against the Lord and against His Anointed'—for truly in this city there were gathered together against Your holy servant Jesus, whom You anointed, both Herod and Pontius Pilate, along with the Gentiles and the peoples of Israel, to do whatever Your hand and Your plan had predestined to take place. And now, Lord, look upon their threats and grant to Your servants to continue to speak Your word with all boldness, while You stretch out Your hand to heal, and signs and wonders are performed through the name of Your holy servant Jesus.'"

he proceeded to arrest Peter also. This was during the days of Unleavened Bread. And when he had seized him, he put him in prison, delivering him over to four squads of soldiers to guard him, intending after the Passover to bring him out to the people. So Peter was kept in prison, but earnest prayer for him was made to God by the church.

Perhaps fearing further arrests, the Christians were praying in a closed house. Answering their prayers, God sent an angel to bring Peter out of prison so that he could continue God's work. Acts 12:6–11 relates,

> Now when Herod was about to bring him out, on that very night, Peter was sleeping between two soldiers, bound with two chains, and sentries before the door were guarding the prison. And behold, an angel of the Lord stood next to him, and a light shone in the cell. He struck Peter on the side and woke him, saying, "Get up quickly." And the chains fell off his hands. And the angel said to him, "Dress yourself and put on your sandals." And he did so. And he said to him, "Wrap your cloak around you and follow me." And he went out and followed him. He did not know that what was being done by the angel was real, but thought he was seeing a vision. When they had passed the first and the second guard, they came to the iron gate leading into the city. It opened for them of its own accord, and they went out and went along one street, and immediately the angel left him. When Peter came to himself, he said, "Now I am sure that the Lord has sent His angel and rescued me from the hand of Herod and from all that the Jewish people were expecting."

Interestingly, the servants were checking people at the door of the house where the Christians were praying, apparently to protect their security. When he arrived, the Christians did not believe it was Peter at the door. Even though the church had turned to God in prayer over this crisis, they apparently did not yet realize that He had answered their prayers.

Regardless of whether hostility came from community religious leaders or from secular government, the church continued its ministry of the Word with vigor. Understanding their role in spreading the Gospel and teaching

God's Word, they thanked God for the honor of suffering for the name of Christ. Realizing what was at stake, rather than asking for relief, they asked for boldness and success in teaching about Jesus. God answered their prayers so that they could speak God's Word with renewed boldness,[15] the church grew as people turned to Christ, and "the word of God increased and multiplied" (Acts 12:24).

Stephen—Martyred for the Faith

> Stephen, full of grace and power, was doing great wonders and signs among the people. . . . And they stirred up the people and the elders and the scribes, and they came upon him and seized him and brought him before the council. (Acts 6:8, 12)

> But they cried out with a loud voice and stopped their ears and rushed together at him. Then they cast him out of the city and stoned him. And the witnesses laid down their garments at the feet of a young man named Saul. And as they were stoning Stephen, he called out, "Lord Jesus, receive my spirit." And falling to his knees he cried out with a loud voice, "Lord, do not hold this sin against them." And when he had said this, he fell asleep. (Acts 7:57–60)

The arrest and stoning of Stephen (Acts 6:8–7:60) presents a different scene of hostility. Stephen was arrested and put on trial based on false accusations simply because of opposition to the Gospel of Jesus Christ.[16] He responded with an inspired defense of his faith (Acts 7:2–53), outlining the

---

15 "And when they had prayed, the place in which they were gathered together was shaken, and they were all filled with the Holy Spirit and continued to speak the word of God with boldness" (Acts 4:31).

16 "And Stephen, full of grace and power, was doing great wonders and signs among the people. Then some of those who belonged to the synagogue of the Freedmen (as it was called), and of the Cyrenians, and of the Alexandrians, and of those from Cilicia and Asia, rose up and disputed with Stephen. But they could not withstand the wisdom and the Spirit with which he was speaking. Then they secretly instigated men who said, 'We have heard him speak blasphemous words against Moses and God.' And they stirred up the people and the elders and the scribes, and they came upon him and seized him and brought him before the council, and they set up false witnesses who said, 'This man never ceases to speak words against this holy place and the law, for we have heard him say that this Jesus of Nazareth will destroy this place and will change the customs that Moses delivered to us'" (Acts 6:8–14).

history of God's dealings with Israel to illustrate His promises and faithfulness in contrast with Israel's stiff-necked rebelliousness.[17] At first glance, we might think that Stephen's defense was a failure (see the outcome related above in Acts 7:57–60). After all, what was the point of his speech to the crowd if not to save his life? Yet apparently it was more important to Stephen to defend and explain God's grace than to try to get himself out of an impending death sentence. In a sense, this was a lot like Shadrach, Meshach, and Abednego's willingness to risk death rather than turn away from God. And the Holy Spirit made Stephen's words so powerful and effective that his executioners had to cover their ears. No doubt God used these words to touch bystanders like Saul, who would a few days later be called to account by the Lord and then renamed Paul. And, in a larger way, God used this crisis point to send His people forth from Jerusalem to take the Gospel to the surrounding nations. This dispersal, or Diaspora, marked the first significant movement taking the Gospel beyond Jerusalem and Judea, and eventually to the ends of the earth.[18]

We often have trouble seeing how God would use a bad situation for good, but leaders of the Early Church set an example for us in believing that God uses all things for His purposes. With this foundation of faith, Peter could write, "To those who are elect exiles of the Dispersion . . . according to the foreknowledge of God the Father, in the sanctification of the Spirit, for obedience to Jesus Christ and for sprinkling with His blood: May grace and peace be multiplied to you" (1 Peter 1:1–2).

Paul—Opposed, Arrested, and Tried

> Five times I received at the hands of the Jews the forty lashes less one. Three times I was beaten with rods. Once I was stoned. Three times I was shipwrecked; a night and a day I was adrift at sea; on frequent journeys, in danger from rivers, danger from

---

17 Acts 7:51–53 records the challenge Stephen posed at the end of his sermon, "You stiff-necked people, uncircumcised in heart and ears, you always resist the Holy Spirit. As your fathers did, so do you. Which of the prophets did your fathers not persecute? And they killed those who announced beforehand the coming of the Righteous One, whom you have now betrayed and murdered, you who received the law as delivered by angels and did not keep it."

18 "And there arose on that day a great persecution against the church in Jerusalem, and they were all scattered throughout the regions of Judea and Samaria, except the apostles" (Acts 8:1).

robbers, danger from my own people, danger from Gentiles, danger in the city, danger in the wilderness, danger at sea, danger from false brothers; in toil and hardship, through many a sleepless night, in hunger and thirst, often without food, in cold and exposure. (2 Corinthians 11:24–27)

He at once took soldiers and centurions and ran down to them. And when they saw the tribune and the soldiers, they stopped beating Paul. Then the tribune came up and arrested him and ordered him to be bound with two chains. (Acts 21:32–33a)

But Paul said, "I am standing before Caesar's tribunal, where I ought to be tried. To the Jews I have done no wrong, as you yourself know very well. If then I am a wrongdoer and have committed anything for which I deserve to die, I do not seek to escape death. But if there is nothing to their charges against me, no one can give me up to them. I appeal to Caesar." Then Festus, when he had conferred with his council, answered, "To Caesar you have appealed; to Caesar you shall go." (Acts 25:10–12)

We should also take note of the varied situations Paul encountered during his missionary travels. As God's man to take the Gospel to Jew and Gentile across the central and northeastern part of the Mediterranean region, Paul was a veritable lightning rod for opposition and physical persecution. Early on, Paul and Barnabas ran into disparate reactions when they shared the Gospel in Antioch of Pisidia: the Gentiles rejoiced but the Jews stirred up the leaders of the community against them, apparently out of jealousy at how the Gospel was meant for all mankind.[19] They drove Paul and Barnabas out of town, but the fact that disciples were left behind showed that God's Word had been planted and was bearing fruit. Next, when Paul and Barnabas

---

19 "And when the Gentiles heard this, they began rejoicing and glorifying the word of the Lord, and as many as were appointed to eternal life believed. And the word of the Lord was spreading throughout the whole region. But the Jews incited the devout women of high standing and the leading men of the city, stirred up persecution against Paul and Barnabas, and drove them out of their district. But they shook off the dust from their feet against them and went to Iconium. And the disciples were filled with joy and with the Holy Spirit" (Acts 13:48–52).

preached the Gospel in Iconium, some of the Jews and some of the Gentiles believed. However, some of those who did not believe tried to stop the ministry and conspired to stone them, so they left town ahead of the mob.[20] In the next town, Lystra, Paul healed a crippled man, but then local pagan priests mistook Paul and Barnabas for Hermes and Zeus. With difficulty, Paul and Barnabas corrected the mistake, but by then parts of the mob from Antioch and Iconium caught up with them (Acts 14:8–18 provides the whole narrative). They stoned Paul and left him for dead, but the following day he was able to go on with Barnabas to the next city.[21]

In Paul's next missionary journey, he and Silas were beaten and jailed in Philippi at least in part because their Gospel ministry deprived some fortune-tellers of their livelihood.[22] They were released from prison the next day, but by then the Philippian jailer and his entire family had received the Gospel and been baptized.[23] When Paul preached in Thessalonica, some of

---

20 "Now at Iconium they entered together into the Jewish synagogue and spoke in such a way that a great number of both Jews and Greeks believed. But the unbelieving Jews stirred up the Gentiles and poisoned their minds against the brothers. So they remained for a long time, speaking boldly for the Lord, who bore witness to the word of His grace, granting signs and wonders to be done by their hands. But the people of the city were divided; some sided with the Jews and some with the apostles. When an attempt was made by both Gentiles and Jews, with their rulers, to mistreat them and to stone them, they learned of it and fled to Lystra and Derbe, cities of Lycaonia, and to the surrounding country, and there they continued to preach the gospel" (Acts 14:1–7).

21 Acts 14:19–20 shows Paul surviving yet another attack, "But Jews came from Antioch and Iconium, and having persuaded the crowds, they stoned Paul and dragged him out of the city, supposing that he was dead. But when the disciples gathered about him, he rose up and entered the city, and on the next day he went on with Barnabas to Derbe."

22 "As we were going to the place of prayer, we were met by a slave girl who had a spirit of divination and brought her owners much gain by fortune-telling. She followed Paul and us, crying out, 'These men are servants of the Most High God, who proclaim to you the way of salvation.' And this she kept doing for many days. Paul, having become greatly annoyed, turned and said to the spirit, 'I command you in the name of Jesus Christ to come out of her.' And it came out that very hour. But when her owners saw that their hope of gain was gone, they seized Paul and Silas and dragged them into the marketplace before the rulers. And when they had brought them to the magistrates, they said, 'These men are Jews, and they are disturbing our city. They advocate customs that are not lawful for us as Romans to accept or practice.' The crowd joined in attacking them, and the magistrates tore the garments off them and gave orders to beat them with rods. And when they had inflicted many blows upon them, they threw them into prison, ordering the jailer to keep them safely. Having received this order, he put them into the inner prison and fastened their feet in the stocks" (Acts 16:16–24). Notice the combination of economic and demonic factors involved in opposing the Gospel.

23 "And the jailer called for lights and rushed in, and trembling with fear he fell down before Paul and Silas. Then he brought them out and said, 'Sirs, what must I do to be saved?' And they said, 'Believe in the Lord Jesus, and you will be saved, you and your household.' And they spoke the word of the Lord to him and to all who were in his house. And he took them the same hour of the night and

the Jews stirred up opposition to the Gospel and provoked physical attacks on Christians. Parenthetically, this is also the first recorded instance where people accused Christians of having "turned the world upside down," which speaks to the magnitude of changes God would bring about through ministry of the Word.[24] Later, Athenians mocked Paul for believing in the resurrection of the dead,[25] and then the Corinthians accused Paul of teaching people to worship God in a way that would break the law.[26] Finally, some of the silversmiths in Ephesus accused Paul of teaching people to worship the one true God rather than worshiping idols and shrines that they made and sold, leading to the craftsmen's loss of business.[27]

Paul encountered harsh words, false accusations, physical abuse, and

washed their wounds; and he was baptized at once, he and all his family" (Acts 16:29–33).

24 "Now when they had passed through Amphipolis and Apollonia, they came to Thessalonica, where there was a synagogue of the Jews. And Paul went in, as was his custom, and on three Sabbath days he reasoned with them from the Scriptures, explaining and proving that it was necessary for the Christ to suffer and to rise from the dead, and saying, 'This Jesus, whom I proclaim to you, is the Christ.' And some of them were persuaded and joined Paul and Silas, as did a great many of the devout Greeks and not a few of the leading women. But the Jews were jealous, and taking some wicked men of the rabble, they formed a mob, set the city in an uproar, and attacked the house of Jason, seeking to bring them out to the crowd. And when they could not find them, they dragged Jason and some of the brothers before the city authorities, shouting, 'These men who have turned the world upside down have come here also, and Jason has received them, and they are all acting against the decrees of Caesar, saying that there is another king, Jesus.' And the people and the city authorities were disturbed when they heard these things" (Acts 17:1–8). As an aside, Christian ministry should still turn the world upside down, but this will inevitably encounter resistance.

25 "Now when they heard of the resurrection of the dead, some mocked. But others said, 'We will hear you again about this'" (Acts 17:32).

26 "But when Gallio was proconsul of Achaia, the Jews made a united attack on Paul and brought him before the tribunal, saying, 'This man is persuading people to worship God contrary to the law.' But when Paul was about to open his mouth, Gallio said to the Jews, 'If it were a matter of wrongdoing or vicious crime, O Jews, I would have reason to accept your complaint. But since it is a matter of questions about words and names and your own law, see to it yourselves. I refuse to be a judge of these things.' And he drove them from the tribunal. And they all seized Sosthenes, the ruler of the synagogue, and beat him in front of the tribunal. But Gallio paid no attention to any of this" (Acts 18:12–17).

27 "About that time there arose no little disturbance concerning the Way. For a man named Demetrius, a silversmith, who made silver shrines of Artemis, brought no little business to the craftsmen. These he gathered together, with the workmen in similar trades, and said, 'Men, you know that from this business we have our wealth. And you see and hear that not only in Ephesus but in almost all of Asia this Paul has persuaded and turned away a great many people, saying that gods made with hands are not gods. And there is danger not only that this trade of ours may come into disrepute but also that the temple of the great goddess Artemis may be counted as nothing, and that she may even be deposed from her magnificence, she whom all Asia and the world worship.' When they heard this they were enraged and were crying out, 'Great is Artemis of the Ephesians!'" (Acts 19:23–28).

threats—sometimes out of jealousy and at least twice because of economic and cultural pressures created by people turning to God. Even though the apparent motives were often mixed, common threads were opposition to the Gospel, Christians, and Christ. Some of these behaviors were rational outcomes of human expectations, pride, and sin, but sometimes the hostility seemed chaotic and almost irrational, as though other forces were at play. This suggests that hostility toward Christians is more than a cultural or social phenomenon; it has deep roots in sin, spiritual warfare waged by the evil one, and the world's opposition to the Christ. God desires all to be saved,[28] but the evil one tries to oppose this at every turn.

Time after time, hostility arose in direct opposition to the spread of the Gospel after the Diaspora. We are effectively part of that Diaspora even today as God continues to place us where He would have us share His Gospel and as hostility continues to rise up against Christians and the Church. A theological understanding of persecution must take into account the effects of sin, the reality of spiritual warfare raging near or sometimes all around God's people, and the ongoing attacks against Christ and His Church until the day when He returns to make all things new. The theological basis for Christian response, or how we handle opposition, will be our next topic of discussion.

⌘ ⌘

---

28 First Timothy 2:3–4 states, "This is good, and it is pleasing in the sight of God our Savior, who desires all people to be saved and to come to the knowledge of the truth."

Discussion Questions

1. The Old Testament and New Testament accounts in this chapter describe several different people of God who encountered bad situations, with hostility or worse. Which person do you most closely identify with, and why?

2. When are you tempted to do what you want instead of what God wants, even though you know better? How do you deal with that temptation?

3. Have you ever experienced God rescuing you from a tough, hostile situation? How so?

4. What do you think was behind the opposition or persecution of Christians that you have seen or experienced?

5. Have you ever experienced what you felt to be a spiritual attack against you as a Christian? How did it turn out?

3

Theological Basis for Christian Response

Hostility and persecution can impact us in many ways. Beneath the layers of physical and emotional challenges, though, are layers of spiritual issues that need attention. Many of these challenges and needs are situational; they vary from case to case and situation to situation. However, we find the answers we need in God's Word, which He uses to assure, comfort, and guide us. On the other hand, these are often general principles that may not speak to our situation as directly as we might like. To drill down to a more specific level of application, we need to know the how and why of things, to know how God would apply His Word to our personal situation. This means that we need to seek God's mind and heart. Knowing God is more helpful and more enlightening than all of the detailed instructions we could ever devise. We need to know His mind, in that we need to know His will, desires, and objectives. In other words, what would He like to see accomplished? And we need to know His heart, in that we need to grasp His love for us

We find the answers we need in God's Word.

and His love for all of humanity to be able to understand His motives. In other words, why would He like this accomplished? Knowing His love but not His will can lead to a misdirected or inappropriate response; knowing His will but not His love can lead to a selfish or insincere response. It should be no surprise, then, that our best response to hostility will be one He designs in keeping with His objectives and His motives.

God's thoughts are higher than our thoughts, and God's ways are not our own.[1] He is omniscient and omnipotent, but we are limited. This means that we can never fully understand God or His plans, but that does not deter God, nor should it deter us from seeking His direction. As Paul describes in his Second Letter to the Corinthians, God puts His grace into jars of clay, meaning us, recognizing that we are limited and fragile.[2] As a friend once told me, we are all cracked pots! Of course, God already understands all this, so He takes steps to help us in our limited and fragile understanding. Rather than leaving us to figure it out on our own, as if we even had any hope of doing so, God reveals His heart and mind most clearly in Jesus Christ. God's mind revealed in Christ tells us what He would like to see done; God's heart revealed in Christ tells us why.

Living in Christ rather than by our own desires or intentions can liberate us from asking, "Why me?" as a paralyzing complaint. Instead, we take a deep breath, step out of ourselves, and ask, "What would God like to accomplish by me being here at this place and time?"[3] Then, enlightened and refocused by God's grace, we take up our cross and step out on the path forward with God's impetus and perspective. Let us be clear: this is not anything we devise or generate to do for God; we have no power to accomplish or even initiate this on our own. This is something we ask God to do for us

---

1   "For My thoughts are not your thoughts, neither are your ways My ways, declares the LORD. For as the heavens are higher than the earth, so are My ways higher than your ways and My thoughts than your thoughts" (Isaiah 55:8–9).

2   "But we have this treasure in jars of clay, to show that the surpassing power belongs to God and not to us. We are afflicted in every way, but not crushed; perplexed, but not driven to despair; persecuted, but not forsaken; struck down, but not destroyed; always carrying in the body the death of Jesus, so that the life of Jesus may also be manifested in our bodies. For we who live are always being given over to death for Jesus' sake, so that the life of Jesus also may be manifested in our mortal flesh" (2 Corinthians 4:7–11).

3   By the way, if we do not have a sense of why we are here and for what purpose, why not put those questions to God? Psalm 139:16 and Ephesians 2:10 both suggest that God has things in mind that He would like to accomplish through us; why not ask?

and through us, and He has a proven track record of making it happen. To begin to understand this dynamic, we need to look at how He uses us as His agents, uses our suffering, gives us resources, and gives our response meaning.

God Works through Us

First and foremost, our approach to hostility must take into account our roles as ambassadors[4] and as the royal priesthood.[5] An ambassador represents one country and its interests to another, and conveys important messages from one to another. People often treat ambassadors with respect, but in some situations people abuse or ignore them. Even so, the ambassadors are still responsible for performing their duties faithfully and are accountable to those whom they represent. We serve as ambassadors between God and those who are not yet part of His kingdom, and as ambassadors we work to ensure clear communication of the Gospel. Sometimes people respect us, while at other times we face hostility or worse. Regardless, we must remain faithful to the One whom we represent. Turning to the other model, priests represent people and their interests (particularly their need for forgiveness) to God and represent God's authority (including the authority to forgive sin) to people. We serve in the role of a royal priesthood between God and humanity, representing God and holding out His grace to those who would receive it. God's love as seen in Jesus Christ necessarily shapes and guides our roles as ambassador and priest.

We do not simply wake up one morning and decide on our own to become an ambassador or decide to join the priesthood of all believers. We cannot simply create or take on such roles on our own or for our own goals. Instead, you might say that we inherit these roles by right of birth; specifically our rebirth into the kingdom of God. Further, these dual roles imply

---

4 "All this is from God, who through Christ reconciled us to Himself and gave us the ministry of reconciliation; that is, in Christ God was reconciling the world to Himself, not counting their trespasses against them, and entrusting to us the message of reconciliation. Therefore, we are ambassadors for Christ, God making His appeal through us. We implore you on behalf of Christ, be reconciled to God" (2 Corinthians 5:18–20).

5 "You are a chosen race, a royal priesthood, a holy nation, a people for His own possession, that you may proclaim the excellencies of Him who called you out of darkness into His marvelous light" (1 Peter 2:9).

an intentional equipping, assignment, and purpose, all of which affect how we live our life, including our vocations, day by day. We are not here by accident; we are here for the work of Christ! The Holy Spirit places us where He wants us to serve; prepares us with godly wisdom, scriptural understanding, and words to say when we need to say them; gives us spiritual gifts for the good of the Church; and directs our steps in keeping with His desire for all to be saved and to come to knowledge of the truth (see our earlier mention of 1 Timothy 2:3–4). Knowing all of this, we strive to run the course He sets before us, even when that course is difficult.

In addition to our roles as God's ambassadors and priests, we each also have a role to play as prophet. This does not mean serving as fortune-tellers. In the Old Testament, God's prophets were men and women who spoke God's Word to the people, kings, and commoners alike. Sometimes these words were messages of peace and comfort, sometimes they were to edify or teach, and often they were words of warning and judgment. The messages called people to turn around and walk with God, and they pointed to God's authority and mercy, reflecting Law and Gospel even before the coming of Jesus. Unfortunately, people often disregarded God's prophets, but this in no way negated God's Word, because God is faithful and His words do not fail. God continues to spread His Word today through our confessions. Acts 2:14–18 tells us,

> Peter, standing with the eleven, lifted up his voice and addressed them: "Men of Judea and all who dwell in Jerusalem, let this be known to you, and give ear to my words. For these people are not drunk, as you suppose, since it is only the third hour of the day. But this is what was uttered through the prophet Joel: 'And in the last days it shall be, God declares, that I will pour out My Spirit on all flesh, and your sons and your daughters shall prophesy, and your young men shall see visions, and your old men shall dream dreams; even on My male servants and female servants in those days I will pour out My Spirit, and they shall prophesy.'"

At Pentecost, we Christians were all given the joy and responsibility of sharing God's Word to our neighbors, and even to those who oppose us. This is a hard yet joyous assignment.

Our motivation, our zeal, begins with God's love for us, and His love for others through us, rather than with any motivation or drive that we could contrive. This is not a case where we can bootstrap ourselves into loving others; no amount of self-motivation, personal-best coaching, or inspirational talks will do the trick. Any love that we think we can conjure up will turn selfish sooner or later, bringing our motivation to a grinding halt. Loving others with God's love is simply too contrary to our sinful nature. So, what to do? We must start by realizing that "God so loved the world . . ." and that even though the world greeted His love with enmity, His love was greater than that enmity. To make it more personal, know that His love is greater than my enmity; His love is greater than our enmity. He loved us while we were still His enemies, and He sent His Son to save us even at the cost of His life.[6] This in no way took God by surprise; Jesus knew even before coming into our world that He would encounter hostility and persecution and ultimately lay down His life for our sake.[7] Now God calls us to take up our cross and follow Jesus, loving those around us sacrificially just as He loves those around us. Jesus laid down His life, paying the ultimate price of redemption, and He may call us to do likewise. We are part of God's plan for reaching the world; we live out God's plan by His love and His enabling.

Jesus said, "Love your enemies,"[8] but this challenges us in two ways: first,

---

6   "For while we were still weak, at the right time Christ died for the ungodly. For one will scarcely die for a righteous person—though perhaps for a good person one would dare even to die—but God shows His love for us in that while we were still sinners, Christ died for us. Since, therefore, we have now been justified by His blood, much more shall we be saved by Him from the wrath of God. For if while we were enemies we were reconciled to God by the death of His Son, much more, now that we are reconciled, shall we be saved by His life" (Romans 5:6–10).

7   Recall that in John 10:14–18, Jesus said, "I am the good shepherd. I know My own and My own know Me, just as the Father knows Me and I know the Father; and I lay down My life for the sheep. And I have other sheep that are not of this fold. I must bring them also, and they will listen to My voice. So there will be one flock, one shepherd. For this reason the Father loves Me, because I lay down My life that I may take it up again. No one takes it from Me, but I lay it down of My own accord. I have authority to lay it down, and I have authority to take it up again. This charge I have received from My Father."

8   In Matthew 5:44–47, during the Sermon on the Mount, Jesus taught, "I say to you, Love your enemies and pray for those who persecute you, so that you may be sons of your Father who is in heaven. For He makes His sun rise on the evil and on the good, and sends rain on the just and on the unjust. For if you love those who love you, what reward do you have? Do not even the tax collectors do the same? And if you greet only your brothers, what more are you doing than others?

how can we love people *we* regard as enemies and, second, how can we love those who regard *us* as enemies? If we see them as enemies, perhaps we need to examine our intentions to be sure that we have the correct understanding. If they see us as enemies, we still must examine ourselves to be sure that we have not caused the problem. In either case, a proper understanding of God's love for them and for us is the best starting point for loving our enemies. This becomes possible as we begin to understand the magnitude of God's love for us. He loved us when we were yet His enemies (see Romans 5:6–10), and certainly well before we held Him in any esteem. Digging deeper, we realize that God expects us to love those around us with His love, impossible though that may seem. Deeper still, this requires a changed life, a life driven by the indwelling Holy Spirit rather than by our self-interested aims and perspectives. To make this possible, God is transforming us into the image of Christ.[9]

With His love driving our thoughts and feelings, we can begin to emulate the mercy of Christ's plea from the cross, asking the Father to forgive those who crucified Him,[10] just as Stephen emulated his Lord when he asked for forgiveness for those who were stoning him.[11] Saturated and motivated by God's love, we strive to show Christ to those who oppose the Lord, His message, and us. As Scripture says in 1 John 4:19, "We love because He first loved us." The more we understand the completely undeserved mercy, love, and grace that God has given us in Christ, the more He enables us to see those around us through His eyes. This includes those who oppose us and even those who persecute us.

As our will and identity become aligned with the will and identity of Jesus Christ, as we become conformed to His image, we begin to participate in His sufferings.[12] This suffering may be part of our situation as we

---

Do not even the Gentiles do the same?"

9   "Now the Lord is the Spirit, and where the Spirit of the Lord is, there is freedom. And we all, with unveiled face, beholding the glory of the Lord, are being transformed into the same image from one degree of glory to another. For this comes from the Lord who is the Spirit" (2 Corinthians 3:17–18).

10   Luke 23:34 records Jesus crying out, "Father, forgive them, for they know not what they do."

11   Acts 7:60 relates Stephen's last statement before he died: "Lord, do not hold this sin against them."

12   First Peter 4:12–14 says, "Beloved, do not be surprised at the fiery trial when it comes upon you to test you, as though something strange were happening to you. But rejoice insofar as you share

work in ministry for salvation[13] or, taking perhaps a larger view, it may be suffering on behalf of the Body of Christ, the Church.[14] Such suffering is not happenstance; God uses it to build our strength and tenacity, much as a smith heats and hammers metal to forge it into a strong, tough new tool. And we are indeed His tools for ministry. God also uses suffering to knock off our rough edges and polish us to better shine with the beauty of Christ, much as a craftsman tumbles precious stones for weeks in a mix of abrasive grit to knock off rough edges, polish their appearance, and bring out their God-given beauty. Tumbling and polishing precious stones is a very slow process, and there are no shortcuts. Indeed, Scripture assures us that God uses suffering to produce endurance, endurance to produce character, character to produce hope, and hope to point us to God's love.[15] He is remaking us, making us more Christlike! But this is not for our glory, it is for the glory of Christ, as He uses us to reach and save our neighbors.

God Uses Our Circumstances

When hostility or persecution close in on us, it might temporarily cloud our vision. We may not be able to see beyond our circumstances, much less see how God is using our suffering. Yet He is with us, and He may be using our situation in ways that lie over the horizon, out of our view. Examples in Scripture show that He indeed uses such situations for

---

Christ's sufferings, that you may also rejoice and be glad when His glory is revealed. If you are insulted for the name of Christ, you are blessed, because the Spirit of glory and of God rests upon you."

13 Second Corinthians 1:5–6 explains, "For as we share abundantly in Christ's sufferings, so through Christ we share abundantly in comfort too. If we are afflicted, it is for your comfort and salvation; and if we are comforted, it is for your comfort, which you experience when you patiently endure the same sufferings that we suffer." The apostle Paul speaks of suffering as he works for the comfort and salvation of the Corinthians; it would be strange if the Corinthians were to experience suffering but never see Paul, Timothy, or other leaders suffer.

14 Colossians 1:24 says, "Now I rejoice in my sufferings for your sake, and in my flesh I am filling up what is lacking in Christ's afflictions for the sake of His body, that is, the church." The apostle Paul speaks of suffering for the Church as a whole, reflecting both his God-given passion for the Gospel and the many difficulties he encountered.

15 Romans 5:3–5 explains, "We rejoice in our sufferings, knowing that suffering produces endurance, and endurance produces character, and character produces hope, and hope does not put us to shame, because God's love has been poured into our hearts through the Holy Spirit who has been given to us."

His purposes. Biblical examples that come to mind include Joseph, Stephen, and Paul.

Joseph

Joseph was detained and sold into slavery by his brothers, rescued to work in Potiphar's household, falsely accused and sent to prison, and finally brought out of prison to become Pharaoh's deputy to rule over Egypt. Every time he thought his situation had stabilized, for good or for bad, it changed! God used these cycles of suffering, rescue, and successful work to bless Potiphar, Pharaoh's baker, Pharaoh and all of Egypt, and finally God's chosen people whom Joseph was able to save from famine. However, what might be less obvious is that He also used them to mature Joseph and temper his faith—compare the young Joseph bragging about his dreams[16] with the mature Joseph forgiving and reassuring his brothers after the death of their father Jacob.[17] At the end of his days, Joseph could bear witness that God meant for good even the evil that they had done, meaning that God had used the evil times as well as the good for the ultimate good of His plans and purposes.

Yet even though Joseph was a man of faith, his faith did not make the pit or the prison any less harsh. It did not shield him from his brothers' envy

---

16 "Now Joseph had a dream, and when he told it to his brothers they hated him even more. He said to them, 'Hear this dream that I have dreamed: Behold, we were binding sheaves in the field, and behold, my sheaf arose and stood upright. And behold, your sheaves gathered around it and bowed down to my sheaf.' His brothers said to him, 'Are you indeed to reign over us? Or are you indeed to rule over us?' So they hated him even more for his dreams and for his words. Then he dreamed another dream and told it to his brothers and said, 'Behold, I have dreamed another dream. Behold, the sun, the moon, and eleven stars were bowing down to me.' But when he told it to his father and to his brothers, his father rebuked him and said to him, 'What is this dream that you have dreamed? Shall I and your mother and your brothers indeed come to bow ourselves to the ground before you?' And his brothers were jealous of him, but his father kept the saying in mind" (Genesis 37:5–11).

17 "When Joseph's brothers saw that their father was dead, they said, 'It may be that Joseph will hate us and pay us back for all the evil that we did to him.' So they sent a message to Joseph, saying, 'Your father gave this command before he died: "Say to Joseph, 'Please forgive the transgression of your brothers and their sin, because they did evil to you.'"' And now, please forgive the transgression of the servants of the God of your father.' Joseph wept when they spoke to him. His brothers also came and fell down before him and said, 'Behold, we are your servants.' But Joseph said to them, 'Do not fear, for am I in the place of God? As for you, you meant evil against me, but God meant it for good, to bring it about that many people should be kept alive, as they are today. So do not fear; I will provide for you and your little ones.' Thus he comforted them and spoke kindly to them" (Genesis 50:15–21).

when they plotted to kill him. It did not protect him from Potiphar's wife's schemes or from being forgotten by Pharaoh's baker when he was released from prison as Joseph had predicted. Joseph suffered multiple difficulties and setbacks, yet God preserved and used him to bless individuals and save entire nations. Even when Joseph first received dreams pointing ahead to a future role of leadership, he could not have imagined the extent to which God would use the setbacks and hostility in his life—even the wrongdoing of his brothers—for good that would affect many generations to come. By God's grace and His gift of faith, Joseph was able to see the hand of God through the bad as well as the good, even though each kind of circumstance has its own distractions and blind spots. And perhaps the final joy Joseph received on this earth was the opportunity to see how God had blessed others through his life.

Stephen

As we discussed in the previous chapter, Stephen, the first martyr, had a record of fruitful service as a deacon in the Early Church (Acts 6:8), but then he was arrested, falsely accused, tried on trumped-up charges, and ultimately stoned to death.[18] From a human point of view, this was a terrible tragedy and the end of a fruitful, productive ministry. He met a bloody end, and this apparently opened the doors to persecution of the Church in Jerusalem. God had already used Stephen as a key leader and one of the first deacons in the Early Church, but then He used his trial as an opportunity for a definitive witness to a people who badly needed to hear God's Law and Gospel. God blessed even more people through Stephen's death than by his life, because the end of Stephen's life triggered the start of the Diaspora, or dispersal, of Christians from Jerusalem[19] to surrounding areas to live out the Great Commission. This dispersal included Philip taking the

---

18 Acts 7 records Stephen's defense, the outrage that arose to interrupt his trial, and the consequent stoning, with Saul as a witness.

19 Acts 8:4 marks the start of the persecution-induced Diaspora that sent people with the Word of God out of Jerusalem and to the ends of the earth. This followed the pattern directed by Jesus in Acts 1:8 when He said, "But you will receive power when the Holy Spirit has come upon you, and you will be My witnesses in Jerusalem and in all Judea and Samaria, and to the end of the earth."

Gospel to Samaria,[20] then to the Ethiopian eunuch,[21] who was treasurer to the queen of Ethiopia, and finally to Caesarea.[22] It also mobilized Saul for action, though not for the action Saul expected! At the end, Stephen was allowed to see heaven open and Jesus standing at the right hand of God, waiting to receive him.[23] His description of what he saw capped off his articulate defense of the faith, and no doubt rang in the ears of his persecutors despite their best attempts to avoid hearing it.

Paul

After Stephen's execution by stoning, Saul began persecuting the Church, but this came to an abrupt end when Jesus stopped him on the road to Damascus. Almost immediately, God pressed the redeemed persecutor, whose name was changed to Paul, into service as church-planter and missionary to the Gentiles.[24] Paul would not have an easy life as Christ's disciple. He suffered in many ways: he carried a personal torment from Satan[25] and, like Joseph, he went through cycles of disaster, hostility, and persecution[26]

---

20 "Now those who were scattered went about preaching the word. Philip went down to the city of Samaria and proclaimed to them the Christ. And the crowds with one accord paid attention to what was being said by Philip when they heard him and saw the signs that he did. For unclean spirits, crying out with a loud voice, came out of many who had them, and many who were paralyzed or lame were healed. So there was much joy in that city" (Acts 8:4–8).

21 "And the eunuch said to Philip, 'About whom, I ask you, does the prophet say this, about himself or about someone else?' Then Philip opened his mouth, and beginning with this Scripture he told him the good news about Jesus. And as they were going along the road they came to some water, and the eunuch said, 'See, here is water! What prevents me from being baptized?' And he commanded the chariot to stop, and they both went down into the water, Philip and the eunuch, and he baptized him. And when they came up out of the water, the Spirit of the Lord carried Philip away, and the eunuch saw him no more, and went on his way rejoicing" (Acts 8:34–39).

22 Acts 8:40 wraps up this part of the narrative with, "But Philip found himself at Azotus, and as he passed through he preached the gospel to all the towns until he came to Caesarea."

23 "But he, full of the Holy Spirit, gazed into heaven and saw the glory of God, and Jesus standing at the right hand of God. And he said, 'Behold, I see the heavens opened, and the Son of Man standing at the right hand of God'" (Acts 7:55–56).

24 The Lord set forth Paul's job description when He sent Ananias to restore Saul's sight. Acts 9:15–16 declares, "[Saul] is a chosen instrument of Mine to carry My name before the Gentiles and kings and the children of Israel. For I will show him how much he must suffer for the sake of My name."

25 Second Corinthians 12:7 mentions Paul's thorn in the flesh: "So to keep me from becoming conceited because of the surpassing greatness of the revelations, a thorn was given me in the flesh, a messenger of Satan to harass me, to keep me from becoming conceited."

26 In 2 Corinthians 11:24–28, Paul explains, "Five times I received at the hands of the Jews the forty lashes less one. Three times I was beaten with rods. Once I was stoned. Three times I was shipwrecked; a night and a day I was adrift at sea; on frequent journeys, in danger from rivers, danger

interspersed with spiritual blessings and success. He no doubt experienced fear, fatigue, pain, and depressing times, yet God gave Paul the encouragement of seeing his work of planting, teaching, and encouraging churches bear fruit over a wide part of the Roman Empire. He was a man driven by the grace of God, and he learned to be content in any situation.[27] God used Paul to build His Church, and rather than letting hostility and persecution stop him, Paul rejoiced in his circumstances.[28]

Paul and Peter each discuss suffering at some length in their letters to the Church, writing with intensity, almost elation, that we might not at first understand. Consider the attitude of an explorer about to venture into a wilderness that will test his survival skills, or a mountain climber about to scale a peak that will test the limits of his ability. They expect to encounter challenges that will give them sore muscles and fatigue, and also place them at risk of hunger, injuries, or even death. Yet they press forward with a hard-to-describe joy for the sake of the goal they hope to achieve. How much more then would joy have described members of the Early Church as they pressed forward with the work and opportunities God prepared for them, with the assurance of the presence of Christ, and with the confidence of His promises? We see this joy of the Early Church throughout the narratives of Acts, and we see it in the opening and closing salutations in many letters of the apostles. We can see this joy today in some of the Christians around us, and perhaps marvel at it, yet their behavior is not strange when we consider the impact of the Holy Spirit indwelling and animating their life. It is not strange when we consider the magnitude of what God has done for us, and

---

from robbers, danger from my own people, danger from Gentiles, danger in the city, danger in the wilderness, danger at sea, danger from false brothers; in toil and hardship, through many a sleepless night, in hunger and thirst, often without food, in cold and exposure. And, apart from other things, there is the daily pressure on me of my anxiety for all the churches." This is a partial menu of the difficulties Paul endured, but it does not mention the significant ridicule, character assassination, and slander that he sometimes met, nor does it mention the difficulties that some of his brothers and sisters in the faith suffered with him.

27   In Philippians 4:11b–13, Paul declares confidently, "I have learned in whatever situation I am to be content. I know how to be brought low, and I know how to abound. In any and every circumstance, I have learned the secret of facing plenty and hunger, abundance and need. I can do all things through Him who strengthens me."

28   In 2 Corinthians 12:10, Paul states, "For the sake of Christ, then, I am content with weaknesses, insults, hardships, persecutions, and calamities. For when I am weak, then I am strong."

that He calls each of us to take up our cross and walk with Him. In Philippians 3:7–14, Paul lays this out for us:

> But whatever gain I had, I counted as loss for the sake of Christ. Indeed, I count everything as loss because of the surpassing worth of knowing Christ Jesus my Lord. For His sake I have suffered the loss of all things and count them as rubbish, in order that I may gain Christ and be found in Him, not having a righteousness of my own that comes from the law, but that which comes through faith in Christ, the righteousness from God that depends on faith—that I may know Him and the power of His resurrection, and may share His sufferings, becoming like Him in His death, that by any means possible I may attain the resurrection from the dead. Not that I have already obtained this or am already perfect, but I press on to make it my own, because Christ Jesus has made me His own. Brothers, I do not consider that I have made it my own. But one thing I do: forgetting what lies behind and straining forward to what lies ahead, I press on toward the goal for the prize of the upward call of God in Christ Jesus.

All of this explains how the heroes of the faith named in Hebrews 11 could persevere: by faith they sensed God with them, and by faith they could see God's kingdom coming into view on the path ahead:

> These all died in faith, not having received the things promised, but having seen them and greeted them from afar, and having acknowledged that they were strangers and exiles on the earth. For people who speak thus make it clear that they are seeking a homeland. If they had been thinking of that land from which they had gone out, they would have had opportunity to return. But as it is, they desire a better country, that is, a heavenly one. Therefore God is not ashamed to be called their God, for He has prepared for them a city. (Hebrews 11:13–16)

God Provides Resources

God works through us, giving us motivation and purpose, and He uses our circumstances to shape us and to achieve His plans. God also provides us with resources to deal with hostility. These resources include His presence, the authority and power entrusted to Jesus, the Holy Spirit who indwells us, and the understanding that God is in control.

We are not left on our own to suffer hostility or persecution; God is alongside us for fellowship and to support and equip us. Think of God's comforting presence to Enoch, father of Methuselah, who "walked with God."[29] Think of the profound assurance that David described in the familiar Twenty-third Psalm, where he describes having our Lord with him through the valley of the shadow of death, and looks ahead to dwelling in the house of the Lord forever. In the stress of the moment, as Elijah found after his conflict with the prophets of Baal on Mount Carmel, it is very easy to think that we are alone and on our own. Yet Elijah found that God had the situation well in hand all along.[30] Our attention is drawn to the crisis rather than to the One who can see us through; this is part of our weak human nature. In fact, Jesus is with us during our entire tenure on the earth and to the end of the age. In the Great Commission recorded in Matthew 28:18–20, He declared, "All authority in heaven and on earth has been given to Me. Go therefore and make disciples of all nations, baptizing them in the name of the Father and of the Son and of the Holy Spirit, teaching them to observe all that I have commanded you. And behold, I am with you always, to the end of the age." His presence gives us peace and assurance under fire, and this even includes "under fire" in a literal sense if we consider the experience of Shadrach, Meshach, and Abednego. It is our great privilege to walk with God, redeemed by Christ. It would serve us well to recall this every morning, asking in prayer simply to walk with Him step by step throughout the day.

> **We are not left on our own to suffer hostility or persecution.**

---

29 Genesis 5:24 tells us, "Enoch walked with God, and he was not, for God took him [directly to heaven]."

30 First Kings 19:18 revealed, much to Elijah's surprise, that "Yet I will leave seven thousand in Israel, all the knees that have not bowed to Baal, and every mouth that has not kissed him."

Jesus declared His authority in heaven and on earth when He announced the Great Commission, and His authority is central to our life and work under those marching orders. This is not a powerless, toothless authority, though. As reported throughout the Gospels, Jesus had already demonstrated His power over illness, injury, handicaps, hunger, winds, storms, demons, and death itself. In fact, during His years of public ministry, Jesus' miracles showed His power over all parts of creation. These signs of power established His credentials, demonstrated His authority, and spoke clearly to believers as well as unbelievers. His is the name above all names, and His presence with us now and "to the end of the age" is active and potent rather than passive and powerless. Working in His name and explicitly under His direction, we have moral authority and spiritual authority that cannot be defeated, even if we suffer persecution and death in the process.

Further, and at Jesus' request, God sends the Holy Spirit to sustain, strengthen, and comfort us. The Spirit gives us words when we need them,[31] He teaches us from the Word,[32] and He is our Helper, dwelling in us.[33] The unambiguous reality of the presence of Christ and the indwelling Holy Spirit fueled the confidence and deliberate boldness exhibited by the disciples following Pentecost. The disciples, who had been cowering in a locked room and dreading the worst, were transformed into fearless witnesses standing and declaring the Gospel of Christ before a crowd of thousands at Pentecost. God did not choose to spare them from beatings, jail, or other forms of suffering, but they were so transformed that they thanked God for the opportunity to suffer for His name. Suffering was really nothing for them compared to the joy of telling others about Jesus. The Holy Spirit can likewise strengthen our faith to see beyond our present circumstances and fix our gaze on the Savior we love.

---

31 Jesus tells His disciples, "When they deliver you over, do not be anxious how you are to speak or what you are to say, for what you are to say will be given to you in that hour. For it is not you who speak, but the Spirit of your Father speaking through you" (Matthew 10:19–20).

32 In John 14:26, Jesus promises, "the Helper, the Holy Spirit, whom the Father will send in My name, He will teach you all things and bring to your remembrance all that I have said to you."

33 In John 14:16–17, Jesus explains, "And I will ask the Father, and He will give you another Helper, to be with you forever, even the Spirit of truth, whom the world cannot receive, because it neither sees Him nor knows Him. You know Him, for He dwells with you and will be in you."

We really need to understand and grasp the idea that God is entirely sovereign; He does not stand back, but actively rules. There is a reason that Scripture calls Him the living God more than twenty-five times; He is living, active, and imminent. He did not create this world just to step back and watch it run; He is actively involved in this world, in my life and in yours. Further, God's support is not just a reaction to whatever the evil one can throw at us; He knows exactly what is coming and is entirely in control. The simple fact remains that God is in charge, and the evil one and our persecutors—despite their lies and bluster—are not. Pilate learned this lesson directly when Jesus looked him in the eye and told him that he had no authority except what had been given him from above.[34] This is a huge source of courage, to know that the One who loves us the most is in complete control of all that we experience, including the bad parts of life. We may not fully understand the situation now, and we may not understand it even until the day God takes us home to heaven, but still we know our sovereign Lord and Savior.

Before moving on to consider some implications of the Gospel as context for our response, let us consider a few other support resources that come from the hand of God. We see that the Holy Spirit works through pastors, teachers, parents, and friends to equip us. He works through our brothers and sisters in Christ to stand beside us for support and encouragement. In fact, we are all part of one body, the Body of Christ.[35] As part of the Body of Christ, we are arranged by God to work together in unison.[36] This

---

34 John 19:10–11 records the moment when Jesus, standing before Pilate, broke His silence and corrected Pilate's understanding of authority: "So Pilate said to him, 'You will not speak to me? Do You not know that I have authority to release You and authority to crucify You?' Jesus answered him, 'You would have no authority over Me at all unless it had been given you from above. Therefore he who delivered Me over to you has the greater sin.'"

35 First Corinthians 12:12–14 states, "For just as the body is one and has many members, and all the members of the body, though many, are one body, so it is with Christ. For in one Spirit we were all baptized into one body—Jews or Greeks, slaves or free—and all were made to drink of one Spirit. For the body does not consist of one member but of many." First Corinthians 12:26–27 reinforces the message, saying, "If one member suffers, all suffer together; if one member is honored, all rejoice together. Now you are the body of Christ and individually members of it."

36 "I therefore, a prisoner for the Lord, urge you to walk in a manner worthy of the calling to which you have been called, with all humility and gentleness, with patience, bearing with one another in love, eager to maintain the unity of the Spirit in the bond of peace. There is one body and one Spirit—just as you were called to the one hope that belongs to your call—one Lord, one faith, one baptism, one God and Father of all, who is over all and through all and in all" (Ephesians 4:1–6).

implies cooperation and coordination and it implies mutual nourishment and support.[37] We will discuss this mutual support briefly in the next few paragraphs and more fully in the next chapter, but for now, let us note that those of us who are in positions that allow us to protect others will certainly need to fulfill that role. More broadly, we each have roles to play, and if we don't perform that service, then, like any unused muscle, we will atrophy and become useless.

So what does this look like in practice? Perhaps the best way to get at this question is to consider how a church protects and supports its members. First and foremost, we pray for one another. We stay in touch with one another; listen to one another's fears, problems, and concerns; and encourage one another with words and with material support. For example, if someone needs food or help with an errand, others in the body step up and provide that help. We look out for one another, and we hold one another's confidences, knowing that we are accountable to our Lord and Savior, Jesus Christ. We know whom we can trust and what kinds of information we can trust them with because rather than trying to live the Christian life solo, we live it together and take a few lumps along the way. For many of us, our congregation is essentially an extended family, and one in which the blood of Christ binds us together closer than anything the world can understand.

Working together in the Body of Christ, we also know, by discernment, experience, or warning, those whom we cannot trust. To the extent possible, we protect one another from the wolves that would ravage our brothers and sisters.[38] We do this by not sharing sensitive information about one another outside the immediate circle of those who need to know.[39] And we do this

---

37 Ephesians 4:15–16 says, "Rather, speaking the truth in love, we are to grow up in every way into Him who is the head, into Christ, from whom the whole body, joined and held together by every joint with which it is equipped, when each part is working properly, makes the body grow so that it builds itself up in love."

38 Documentary films of wolf behavior often show how wolves try to get an animal away from the rest of the herd (or flock) before closing in for the kill. This illustrates why it is so dangerous for a Christian to drift away from the church. Hebrews 10:24–25 advises, "And let us consider how to stir up one another to love and good works, not neglecting to meet together, as is the habit of some, but encouraging one another, and all the more as you see the Day drawing near." This is not to be taken lightly, particularly when we face hostility, oppression, or persecution.

39 For example, if terrorist organizations were scrutinizing our church websites to identify the names and locations of missionaries who might be vulnerable to attack, we would take steps to protect that information. This happens more often than you might think.

by reaching out to one another with a strong hand of support and encouragement in the face of adversity.

In addition to providing brothers and sisters in Christ who support us with fellowship and mutual aid, God may sometimes support us with unexpected allies in difficult circumstances. For example, when the disciples tried to stop an outsider from casting out demons in the name of Jesus, our Lord brought them up short. In Mark 9:39–40, He said, "Do not stop him, for no one who does a mighty work in My name will be able soon afterward to speak evil of Me. For the one who is not against us is for us." This probably took the disciples by surprise. And when Paul's opponents hauled him into court in Achaia, the proconsul Gallio unexpectedly dismissed his case. Acts 18:12–16 relates,

> But when Gallio was proconsul of Achaia, the Jews made a united attack on Paul and brought him before the tribunal, saying, "This man is persuading people to worship God contrary to the law." But when Paul was about to open his mouth, Gallio said to the Jews, "If it were a matter of wrongdoing or vicious crime, O Jews, I would have reason to accept your complaint. But since it is a matter of questions about words and names and your own law, see to it yourselves. I refuse to be a judge of these things." And he drove them from the tribunal.

Examples like these suggest that we should be open and discerning to receive unlikely support or even unexpected allies. Some may be believers who can provide fellowship, some may be unbelievers willing to make a common cause to support our position in the face of controversy,[40] and some may even be people God uses without them ever fully understanding God's hand in what they do.[41]

---

40 See Matthew Harrison, "Free Exercise of Religion: Putting Beliefs into Practice, An Open Letter from Religious Leaders in the United States to All Americans," June 21, 2012, (available at www.lcms.org/hhsmandate).

41 For example, Ezra 6:1–4 says, "Then Darius the king made a decree, and search was made in Babylonia, in the house of the archives where the documents were stored. And in Ecbatana, the citadel that is in the province of Media, a scroll was found on which this was written: 'A record. In the first year of Cyrus the king, Cyrus the king issued a decree: Concerning the house of God at Jerusalem, let the house be rebuilt, the place where sacrifices were offered, and let its foundations be retained. Its height shall be sixty cubits and its breadth sixty cubits, with three layers of great stones and one

Last but perhaps greatest, God feeds and supports us through His Means of Grace: Word and Sacrament. The sacraments of Baptism and the Lord's Supper bind us to Him and restore us in His grace. We receive the Word of God through preaching, teaching, and Bible study, which are crucial to understanding the heart and mind of God. As Jesus said in Matthew 4:4, "Man shall not live by bread alone, but by every word that comes from the mouth of God." And in John 15:5, He said, "I am the vine; you are the branches. Whoever abides in Me and I in him, he it is that bears much fruit, for apart from Me you can do nothing." God gives us these resources and nourishment, and He roots our life in Christ; otherwise, we will not survive.

Response Rooted in the Gospel

How we respond to hostility or persecution inevitably carries implications for the Gospel. When we face hostility, should we retreat, hunker down for survival, or see our situation as an opportunity?[42] If it is an opportunity, then an opportunity to what end? To properly answer this question, we need to step back and take into account God's zeal to reach and save the world. John 3:16 says, "For God so loved the world, that He gave His only Son, that whoever believes in Him should not perish but have eternal life." Think about this familiar declaration in conjunction with 1 Timothy 2:4, which says, "[God] desires all people to be saved and to come to the knowledge of the truth." This really spells out God's priorities for us as we consider the big picture. We may not be able to see it all from our frame of reference (limited by time scale, geographic scale, or perhaps both), but God will use all kinds of circumstances, including hostile situations, to reach out to individuals, neighborhoods, or even entire nations.

---

layer of timber. Let the cost be paid from the royal treasury.'" Ezra 6:6–7, 12 then says, "Now therefore, Tattenai, governor of the province Beyond the River, Shethar-bozenai, and your associates the governors who are in the province Beyond the River, keep away. Let the work on this house of God alone. Let the governor of the Jews and the elders of the Jews rebuild this house of God on its site. . . . May the God who has caused His name to dwell there overthrow any king or people who shall put out a hand to alter this, or to destroy this house of God that is in Jerusalem. I Darius make a decree; let it be done with all diligence." While it is not clear how much Cyrus and Darius knew about God, He clearly used them in His plans for the Jews.

42   If we suffer hostility or persecution, this question is immediate and personal, but it can also distract from the larger picture. If we suffer for Christ or the Gospel, the question is not about us; rather, it should be about how our Lord would use us in these circumstances to reach out to those around us in His name. Note that He is the One reaching out; this is not something that we contrive. *A difficulty for us may often be a mission opportunity for Him.*

In the Old Testament, God used the punishment of Jerusalem as a witness to the nations, but Ezekiel's audience probably did not see it that way until he explained it[43] (and maybe not even then). Why would God use Jerusalem's exile as a witness, and to what end? Observers could see God's power, sovereignty, and righteousness in His judgment of Jerusalem, and they could see His mercy in that He preserved a remnant (even if by exile) from destruction. If this reminded heathen observers that the God who rescued Israel from Egypt centuries earlier was still around and active among the nations, then it could also remind them of the law written within their hearts and it could help call them to seek God's mercy. All of this reflects God's love for the world and His desire that as many as possible receive His grace. He is a missionary God, and He cares deeply about those not yet saved.

Much later, God used the Diaspora of believers from Jerusalem to spread the Gospel, with persecution as an impetus for Christians to leave Jerusalem and take the Gospel to Samaria and the ends of the earth. Witness borne of the Spirit attracts hostility from those still in rebellion against God, but God will use our response to their hostility to provide further witness even if we may not immediately see His hand in our situation. The first-century Christians probably did not immediately see the hand of God in their departure from Jerusalem but moved out in faith anyway, knowing that they were in God's care. They may not have fully understood what was happening, but they continued to trust God as shown by their ongoing witness. Acts 8:4 relates, "Now those who were scattered went about preaching the word." Their example illustrates how we can remain faithful as we continue working through difficult circumstances under God's sovereignty and providence.

Looking back across history, the persecuted Church was sometimes the growing Church, as people turned to God for strength and relief, lived out their reliance on God in front of friends and neighbors, and shared the

---

43 God used Israel as a warning to the surrounding nations in Ezekiel 5:15 ("You shall be a reproach and a taunt, a warning and a horror, to the nations all around you, when I execute judgments on you in anger and fury, and with furious rebukes—I am the LORD; I have spoken"), and as a witness in Ezekiel 20:41 ("As a pleasing aroma I will accept you, when I bring you out from the peoples and gather you out of the countries where you have been scattered. And I will manifest My holiness among you in the sight of the nations"); 36:36 ("Then the nations that are left all around you shall know that I am the LORD; I have rebuilt the ruined places and replanted that which was desolate. I am the LORD; I have spoken, and I will do it"); and 37:27–28 ("My dwelling place shall be with them, and I will be their God, and they shall be My people. Then the nations will know that I am the LORD who sanctifies Israel, when My sanctuary is in their midst forevermore").

Gospel of Jesus Christ wherever they went. Even those Christians who became martyrs under false accusation often boldly confessed God's truth to their jailers and executioners. In this they followed the example of Paul, who wrote of being poured out like a drink offering[44] even as he continued to exhort, encourage, and witness. The situation was often nuanced, though, as the persecuted Church was not without apostates. Further, the apparent church membership may have dwindled while the number of actual members grew as Christians went into hiding. Sometimes persecution completely overwhelmed the Church, and the local church went underground or even disappeared entirely. If this happens to us, we must endure and echo the martyrs in saying, "Thy will be done."

Learning from the past, we see that God uses the stress of a situation on personal levels as well as on community or even larger scales. He may preserve a remnant of believers in a given area or location, or He may not, but we are still part of His overarching plans to save as many as possible. As we conform to Christ, as Christ lives in us, we follow Him along this sacrificial path and count it all as joy along the way. We are part of an intricate tapestry, created by God across time, where local details are important to the bigger picture, and the bigger picture is important to the local details.

In this context, we should reconsider some fundamental characteristics of our position as Christians in society. In the Sermon on the Mount, Jesus pointed out that we serve as salt and light for this world.[45] This service comes with our assigned roles, or vocations, in the realms of church, community, family, and work. This is why we cannot simply turn and run away from the playing field; the playing field is all of life! We are not here by coincidence, but placed as His ambassadors for the Gospel wherever the Holy Spirit sends us. Until He takes us home to heaven, we will serve as salt and light, often without even realizing it at the time.

---

44 "For I am already being poured out as a drink offering, and the time of my departure has come. I have fought the good fight, I have finished the race, I have kept the faith. Henceforth there is laid up for me the crown of righteousness, which the Lord, the righteous judge, will award to me on that Day, and not only to me but also to all who have loved His appearing" (2 Timothy 4:6–8).

45 "You are the salt of the earth, but if salt has lost its taste, how shall its saltiness be restored? It is no longer good for anything except to be thrown out and trampled under people's feet. You are the light of the world. A city set on a hill cannot be hidden. Nor do people light a lamp and put it under a basket, but on a stand, and it gives light to all in the house. In the same way, let your light shine before others, so that they may see your good works and give glory to your Father who is in heaven" (Matthew 5:13–16).

Jesus used practical metaphors to make the lesson easier to grasp. If we are to serve as salt and light, though, it will help to understand what salt and light do. At the time of Christ, salt was a seasoning or commodity. It was costly and it was rare enough that it was conserved, fought over, protected, and sometimes even used for trade or payment. Practical day-to-day uses for salt included preserving food, curing meat, and adding flavor. This suggests that Christians help preserve society, cure its inherent rawness, and add a savory flavor to community life. Indeed, we *are* salt, a valuable commodity that He invests to influence those around us. So of course the choices we make in responding to tough times have a direct impact on our influence as salt.

Light is a rich but rather different metaphor. Light reveals things that were previously in the dark and helps us avoid danger. In another sense, it reveals the truth or perhaps shows the true state of affairs. Jesus is the light of the world, and His light indwells and shines through us. As we convey or perhaps reflect His presence, we serve as light to share His love and His truth with our neighbors. We also serve as light by speaking God's truth, even if opposed, to enlighten the world around us.

Earlier we mentioned our service as salt and light in connection with our vocations. Our vocations provide practical ways or venues for us to interact with family, friends, and neighbors near and far, and our influence as salt and light shows up in those interactions. But what are our vocations?

God gives each of us vocations in which we serve others in our church, community, family, and work. In a sense we are "masks of God" in that God works unseen through us to provide that service.[46] To realize the implications and potential impact of these vocations, consider another metaphor our Lord used: a small amount of yeast in a large amount of dough.[47] We proclaim our Lord and influence those around us by word and deed, by the Word and by acts of mercy. God is the motivating power behind what we do, so just as a small amount of yeast affects an entire loaf of bread, our influence may be much larger than we might expect. We may or may not have opportunities to speak out by preaching, teaching, or simply sharing

---

46 See Gene Edward Veith, *God at Work: Your Christian Vocation in All of Life* (Wheaton, IL: Crossway, 2002).

47 In Matthew 13:33, Jesus taught, "The kingdom of heaven is like leaven that a woman took and hid in three measures of flour, till it was all leavened."

His Word, but we will always have small but significant opportunities to influence those around us by living out His Word in our vocations.

We live in the world but not of the world, and people can see this. God calls us to be faithful, and faithful individuals as well as groups of Christians can have a disproportionately large impact wherever they live. Our level of understanding may not be as complete as we would like, and we can rarely see the whole picture. Seeing the situation from God's point of view, though, starts to give us a sense of that larger picture and sets the stage for us to serve Him as we consider how to respond to hostility.

We may ask, "Why do we encounter hostility?" But it may be more useful to ask, "How would God like to use us in hostile circumstances?" The first question can lapse into a "why me" kind of whining, but the second question is more unsettling because it suggests that God, who loves us, permits us to suffer. It is unsettling because it implies that our comfort might not be the most important consideration in God's plans, and because it hints that God has allowed or may even have caused our discomfort. The only real answer to being unsettled, though, is to be settled in faith in God.

We cannot second-guess the mind of God, but several possibilities might help explain God's intentions for our difficulties: Our discomfort, even our suffering, might be part of a larger witness to neighbors to help them learn of God's justice, love, and forgiveness. Our discomfort might be related to God pushing us out of our situational or geographic comfort zone, moving us into situations or locations where He would like to put our time, energy, and witness to use. Our discomfort could be linked to God's desire to smooth off our rebellious rough spots, discipline us, shape us, and grow us in godliness, love, and dependence upon Him. Ultimately, we must see that our discomfort is part of following in the footsteps of Christ: Jesus came to a hostile world bearing God's love and was crucified. He knew that this would happen; the sacrifice of Christ was God's plan all along. Now He chooses to allow each of us to serve as a little Christ (or Christian) to bear God's love to this hostile world. We take up our cross to fulfill this lovingly sacrificial role, and our response to hostility is indeed rooted in the Gospel of Jesus Christ.

⌘ ⌘

Discussion Questions

1. How are you likely to first react when facing hostility as a Christian? What kind of response would be good for our credibility, presence, and witness?

2. What kinds of vocations do you have, and how do they provide an opportunity to serve or to share your faith with your neighbor?

3. Has God ever used bad situations in your life for your benefit or for His glory? How so?

4. If you encounter persecution, what should you pray instead of asking, "Why me?"?

5. What do you think God's top priority is for your life? How would this affect the way you handle hostility or persecution?

4

Christian Response: Spiritual Disciplines

Hostility toward Christians and the Church can arise in many different ways, and we need godly discernment and understanding to know how best to respond. The key issue, though, comes around to the question of which response best serves to reach our neighbor with the Gospel. God placed us here as His emissaries, so which response best suits His purposes? Our response to hostility or persecution needs to reflect an intentional, proactive approach that follows and relies on our Lord rather than a reactive approach that follows or relies on self or on self-interest. Relying on self courts disaster; relying on our Lord ensures success, though not necessarily success in any worldly sense of the term. The world's values are not God's values.

Regardless of our specific situation or course of action, Christian response should include a combination of spiritual disciplines, such as prayer, self-examination, forgiveness, witness, and support for our brothers and sisters in Christ. And, of course, we need to know what we believe and where we stand, based on God's living yet unchanging Word. Beyond that, we have at our disposal a number of scriptural options in addition to simply turning the other cheek. Depending on the circumstances, we could invoke our rights of citizenship, disengage from the situation, play defense, step up our proclamation of Christ, make common cause with potential allies, or perhaps even leave for another location. Or we may simply suffer and endure. Some of these options are mutually exclusive, while others might be executed in combination.

In this chapter, we will lay out a few hypothetical and actual, real-world examples of hostility, oppression, and persecution to set the stage for discussing our path forward. Then we will consider spiritual disciplines that should undergird how we navigate difficult situations. Discipline is never easy. On the other hand, discipline implies preparation and perseverance. Godly discipline, along with His grace, will see us through. In our practical approach, we will consider how to implement each discipline, discuss some examples where appropriate, and touch on the value of follow-through as well as potential impacts of not following through. Then, in the chapter that follows, we will explore several scriptural options for active or passive response.

Consider a few examples of hostility, oppression, or persecution, any of which might one day affect you, your congregation, or perhaps your Christian brothers and sisters elsewhere:

- You comment about Christian teaching on a website or on social media. Someone objects to what you shared and brands your words as hate speech. Under pressure, and without warning, the company that hosts the website or social media decides to block or close your account because of the allegations. This happened to a pastor and his group in Los Angeles early in 2013[1] when they spoke online about abortion. Twitter froze them out of their accounts, reinstating them upon request a few hours later, but then shut them down for several days when they continued to speak about abortion's effects on the black community.

---

1   Whitney Williams, "Twitter mutes pro-life group ahead of rally," *WORLD News Group*, February 14, 2013.

- Activists learn that you believe homosexuality is a sin, as related in Romans 1:18–32 (just as you believe John 3:16) and start picketing your congregation on Sunday mornings. When your congregation applies for a building permit to expand its facilities, activists lobby the local zoning commission to deny the permit on the basis of accusations that traffic and parking around your church will become a public nuisance. This example actually combines two kinds of real-life events: protests against a congregation in Michigan[2] and instances where church building plans were frustrated by the objections of a few people living in that part of town.[3]

- The public university bars your Christian group from campus unless you agree to allow atheists or people from other (i.e., non-Christian) religions to be elected as student leaders of your Christian group. Muslim groups are acceptable because they are ethnic, and Yoga groups are acceptable because they claim to be health related. However, Christian groups are barred because they are not open to non-Christian leadership. Anecdotal evidence suggests that this kind of discrimination against Christian groups on college campuses has been around for decades. However, since most students graduate and leave after a few years, the administrators and bureaucrats who discriminate against them can simply wait and run out the clock so that the problems often go unreported and uncorrected. More recently, though, an increasing number of universities (e.g., Bowdoin College, Tufts University, Vanderbilt University, and all nineteen campuses of the California State University system) are simply publishing and implementing policies that discriminate against religious groups

---

2   "Gay activists disrupt Sunday service at Michigan church," *Catholic News Agency*, November 13, 2008.

3   A search online for the words "church expansion plans denied" will turn up instances of church plans being frustrated in many different parts of the United States, sometimes for substantive cause but often for reasons such as street parking, traffic congestion, or even because people object to changing landscaping around the church. For example, see "Livermore church expansion plan denied by Alameda County," *Contra Costa Times*, October 3, 2006.

in general and sometimes against Christian groups in particular, so the problem seems to be growing.[4]

- Your Christian college is accused of hatred and bias and then threatened with loss of accreditation because its written statement of faith endorses the authority of God's Word, the Bible, even though admission to the college does not require students to agree with the statement of faith, or even to profess Christianity. This kind of oppression is in play at several different colleges and universities in the United States and Canada, including Trinity Western University in Canada and Gordon College in the U.S.[5] Although Gordon College seems to have won a reprieve, the threat of loss of accreditation has a chilling effect on the college, faculty, donors, current and potential students, and its academic freedom.

- Your employer finds out through an anonymous third person that you support biblical views of marriage. Or perhaps someone tells him that your name is on a list of donors to a political campaign in support of heterosexual marriage. Your employer requires you to participate in sensitivity training in which orthodox Christian, Jewish, and Muslim views of marriage and sexuality are rejected in favor of more "inclusive" values. You are later denied a promotion because you are perceived as not inclusive enough as a manager, and eventually you are pressured to resign from your job because inclusivity and multicultural values have become part of the performance criteria for employment. Variations of

---

4   Emily Belz, "Sent packing," *WORLD News Group*, October 31, 2014; Andrew Walker, "Poll: Church Leaders Predict Repression over Objections To Gay Coupling," *The Federalist*, September 2, 2014; and Josh Good, "The D-word is coming to a campus near you," *WORLD News Group*, October 11, 2014. However, sometimes these situations can be negotiated. For example, see Sarah Padbury, "InterVarsity's Lesson in Effectively Engaging a Secular Culture," *WORLD News Group*, June 26, 2015.

5   J. C. Derrick, "Canadian education minister revokes approval for Christian law school," *WORLD News Group*, December 12, 2014; Joy Pullmann, "What's Happening To Gordon College Is Just The Beginning," *The Federalist*, July 18, 2014; and Leigh Jones, "Review board: Gordon College accreditation not at risk," *WORLD News Group*, March 27, 2015.

this scenario have arisen and are in play in parts of the United States where individuals have chosen to support new initiatives as well as existing laws protecting traditional marriage, or have objected to supporting gay marriage.[6]

- Government agents arrive at your church to remove the cross from atop the steeple. You ask higher officials to intervene, but they ignore your request. When your pastor and a handful of laypeople gather for prayer in front of the local police station, they are arrested and the pastor sentenced to one year in jail for disturbing the peace. This has happened to the Christian Church in some parts of China, where churches exist in what amounts to a two-tiered system. Churches that register with the government are officially recognized and approved, but there is a second tier of churches (including the "underground church") that operates without submitting to the communist authorities. Some areas of China are more tolerant of unregistered congregations than other areas, but this is subject to change. In the Zhejiang province of eastern China, for example, it was acceptable for unregistered congregations to have church buildings, even with crosses atop their steeples. However, the situation changed recently and authorities began removing crosses from churches. When a pastor protested the action and tried to organize prayers for China and for the local government, he was arrested and jailed.[7]

- Members of another (non-Christian) religion start a riot, storm the offices of your Christian organization, and disrupt your

---

6   Examples can be found in Emily Belz, "A clerk's struggle," *WORLD News Group*, April 18, 2015; Marvin Olasky, "Cultural hardball," *WORLD News Group*, April 4, 2015; Michael Cochrane, "Navy denies chaplain's request for religious accommodation," *WORLD News Group*, March 18, 2015; Leigh Jones, "Former Atlanta fire chief sues city for religious discrimination," *WORLD News Group*, February 18, 2015; Nick Eicher, "In Canada, it's career vs. conviction for some Christians," *WORLD News Group*, January 30, 2015; Andrée Seu Peterson, "Pink slip speech," *WORLD News Group*, February 21, 2014; and Bradley R. E. Wright, "Your Faith Might Cost You Your Next Job," *ChristianityToday.com*, June 18, 2014.

7   June Cheng, "China's crackdown on the cross spreads," *WORLD News Group*, August 1, 2014; June Cheng, "Wenzhou pastor sentenced to a year in prison," *WORLD News Group*, March 25, 2015.

meetings. When you call the police, they come and arrest you and other Christians rather than your attackers. Local authorities are reluctant to investigate or prosecute the offenders, perhaps because higher government leaders are members of that religion. While not an everyday occurrence, this kind of behavior has started to happen more frequently in India as that country considers laws to make it illegal for Hindus to convert to Christianity, Islam, or any other religion.[8]

- A militant group invades your village, kills the Christian men, and kidnaps Christian women and children to sell into slavery. The government is not able to protect your village or rescue the kidnapped people. A few kidnap victims escape and report the horrendous situation of the other hostages, but as weeks and months go by, the news media and other countries lose interest and seem to forget about the victims. This is an ongoing problem in northern Nigeria and adjacent Niger, as Boko Haram continues its raids and kidnappings. Although the mainstream news media rarely report on the spiritual dimension of this conflict, Boko Haram aims to impose Muslim Shariah law on the territory it controls, and Christians have often borne the brunt of the violence.[9]

- A family member is kidnapped and later executed by a religious militant group because he is a Christian and refuses to convert to another faith, even under duress. Local, national, and international authorities seem helpless to intervene, and governments that do not support religious freedom do not even see this as a religious or human rights issue. This happens from time to time in Africa and the Middle East, but often goes unreported, at least

---

8   Julia A. Seymour, "Christmas isn't over yet, and neither is holiday persecution," *WORLD News Group*, January 5, 2015; Julia A. Seymour, "India's Christians protest after St. Sebastian's Church burns," *WORLD News Group*, December 8, 2014; and Suryatapa Bhattacharya, "Christians Say Break-In a Sign of Rising Religious Intolerance in Delhi," *The Wall Street Journal*, February 3, 2015.

9   Drew Hinshaw and Gbenga Akingbule, "Boko Haram Rampages, Slaughters in Northeast Nigeria," *The Wall Street Journal*, January 9, 2015; Mary Reichard, "Christians in Niger return home after violent Muslim rampage," *WORLD News Group*, January 29, 2015; and Jamie Dean, "The Lost Girls," *WORLD News Group*, May 31, 2014.

in U.S. news media. The handling of these situations changed, at least temporarily, when the Islamic State (ISIS, or ISIL) beheaded twenty-one Coptic Christians in Libya. Even then, U.S. government officials and news media were reluctant to admit that it was Christians who were being martyred for their faith.[10]

- A new theocratic (i.e., religious) government comes to power through military conquest and marks the homes and businesses of known Christians for special attention at a later date. Meanwhile, they take over church buildings and start using them as military barracks and supply depots. As they sweep back through conquered areas, they return to the marked homes and businesses, torture and execute some Christians, send others into exile or refugee camps, confiscate property, and demand that any Christians who remain pay a special tax for holding to their faith. This is happening today as civil war, fighting between Sunni and Shia branches of Islam, and battles for conquest and control rage across much of Iraq and Syria. Christians caught in the middle face agonizing choices between staying and risking death or fleeing as refugees.[11]

Unfortunately, this is not an exhaustive catalog of bad things happening to Christians in the United States and worldwide. It is only a short representative list, and figuratively speaking, it is the small tip of a large iceberg. Footnoted news articles provide more details about the actual events behind these examples. But if you were to become caught up in one of these kinds of situations, what would you do? And, remembering the Golden Rule, what would you like your fellow Christians to do to support you?

What would you do?

---

10   Mindy Belz, "ISIS beheads 21 Christians, Egypt strikes back," *WORLD News Group*, February 16, 2015; and Jamie Dean, "The ISIS war against 'the people of the cross,'" *WORLD News Group*, February 17, 2015.

11   Tamara Audi, "Iraqi Christians' Dilemma: Stay or Go?" *The Wall Street Journal*, September 29, 2014; Leslie Loftis, "Don't Close Your Eyes To Christians Purged and Tortured in Iraq," *The Federalist*, August 1, 2014; and Rob Schwarzwalder, "Who Is Speaking For The Persecuted Christians In Iraq?" *The Federalist*, August 15, 2014.

Prayer

The first-century church typically responded to crisis with sober-minded prayer. For example, Acts 1:14 tells us that when the apostles were wondering what to do next after Jesus' ascension, "all these with one accord were devoting themselves to prayer, together with the women and Mary the mother of Jesus, and His brothers." Later, when the authorities arrested Peter and John and ordered them to stop speaking in the name of Jesus, the church immediately turned to God in prayer:

> Sovereign Lord, who made the heaven and the earth and the sea and everything in them, who through the mouth of our father David, Your servant, said by the Holy Spirit, "Why did the Gentiles rage, and the peoples plot in vain? The kings of the earth set themselves, and the rulers were gathered together, against the Lord and against His Anointed"—for truly in this city there were gathered together against Your holy servant Jesus, whom You anointed, both Herod and Pontius Pilate, along with the Gentiles and the peoples of Israel, to do whatever Your hand and Your plan had predestined to take place. And now, Lord, look upon their threats and grant to Your servants to continue to speak Your word with all boldness, while You stretch out Your hand to heal, and signs and wonders are performed through the name of Your holy servant Jesus. (Acts 4:24b–30)

Acts 4:31 tells us what happened next: "And when they had prayed, the place in which they were gathered together was shaken, and they were all filled with the Holy Spirit and continued to speak the word of God with boldness." Still later, Acts 12:5 relates that after Peter's arrest by Herod, "Peter was kept in prison, but earnest prayer for him was made to God by the church."[12] Following this pattern, each time a crisis arose, the church turned to God in prayer immediately rather than as an afterthought.

---

12   This third example is particularly valuable because it shows God honoring His people's prayers even when they are rattled and distraught. They were so distraught, in fact, that when God sent an angel to stage a jailbreak for Peter (Acts 12:6–10), apparently in answer to their prayers, they did not believe that Peter was at the door when he showed up at their prayer meeting (Acts 12:14–15).

Prayer is a good starting point for any Christian response to hostility or persecution.[13] Sometimes we might say, "Well, I guess there is nothing we can do except pray about it," as if we have run out of options and praying is our last resort. Why not resort to prayer first? Prayer is a normal, healthy part of our spiritual life.[14] Just as we breathe more often and more deeply when our bodies work harder, we should pray more often and more deeply as we work through hard situations of hostility or persecution.

How then should we go about praying? Volumes have been written on this topic, so we will only touch on a few essentials here. We might pray with fellow Christians in small groups or in a congregational prayer vigil, or we might pray individually. Regardless, it will help if we deliberately set aside some quality time for prayer, if we can find a place to pray that helps us avoid distractions, and if we can be diligent in our praying. Mark 1:35 gives us some insight into how our Lord prayed when it relates, "And rising very early in the morning, while it was still dark, He departed and went out to a desolate place, and there He prayed." We get the impression that Jesus prayed early and often, and as part of His overall approach to living in accord with the Father's will. We should strive to do likewise, particularly as we face challenging times. This regular practice provides a context for spontaneous, on-the-spot prayers as we walk with our Lord through each hour and each day.

What might we pray? The answer to this question might not be as obvious as simply praying for relief from hostility. For example, as described previously, the Islamic State (ISIS) has been persecuting and executing Christians in Iraq, Libya, and Syria. Should we pray for their defeat or for their conversion to Christianity? The answer might be yes—pray for both! Should we pray for God to raise up an evangelist to the Muslims from among them, perhaps in some way similar to how God stopped Saul and restarted his life as Paul, evangelist to the Gentiles? Yes, as God gives us the ability to see the big picture and understand His desires, we should indeed pray for such a miraculous turnaround.

---

13 In fact, Christian leaders worldwide are calling the Church to prayer on behalf of the persecuted Church, as reported in Lynde Langdon, "Christian leaders unite in call to prayer for persecuted church," *WORLD News Group*, February 20, 2015.

14 See The Commission on Theology and Church Relations, *Theology and Practice of Prayer: A Lutheran View* (St. Louis: The Lutheran Church—Missouri Synod, 2012).

Is there anything we should not pray? Strange as it might seem, there are times, particularly in public, congregational, group, or prayer chain settings, when we might need to be careful about the specifics of our prayers. Some people and groups that seek to oppose or harm Christians look for identities and locations of missionaries, pastors, teachers, and even lay people because these might be new targets for hostility. We can and should pray for these people, but we need to be careful not to share too many specifics in open prayers or, for that matter, in email or on social media.

Upon reflection, and with these cautions in mind, we realize that several different kinds of prayer and prayer topics are likely to be appropriate, depending on the situation:

- Prayers anticipating the possibility of hostility or oppression, often intercessory and perhaps broader and more forward-looking than what we normally practice. We can pray for our government, rulers, leaders, enemies, neighbors, and our brothers and sisters in Christ. We can pray for peace; for strength to respond with joy in Christ; for openings to profess our faith; for protection from hostility that we see coming our way; for relief from hostility already experienced; for God's grace, forgiveness, and salvation for our enemies; and for our own wisdom and discernment.

- Situational prayers of petition on behalf of family, congregation, or ourselves, and prayed in real time as we deal with specific events or personal circumstances.

- Expressive prayer, to vent or to deal with feelings as we look to God for salvation and peace. This may not be the kind of prayer that first comes to mind when we think about how to go to our Lord in prayer, but some of the Psalms (e.g., Psalms 3, 7, and 18) reflect exactly this kind of prayer by David, a man after God's own heart.

- Petition and supplication, simply praying for God's strength, patience, wisdom, and discernment to know what to do and what not to do.

Above all, we must be honest in prayer and stay in touch with our Lord as He leads us forward. Staying in touch means time spent in prayer, speaking with Him and waiting on Him, and it means time spent in God's Word, learning His heart and mind. These regular spiritual disciplines are necessary for our strength and mutual support, for discerning God's will, and for seeing the situation and people involved through God's eyes. These disciplines also help order our thoughts and comfort our hearts in troubled situations, help keep our focus on Jesus rather than on self, help fix our attention on the kingdom of God[15] rather than our circumstances, and help reinforce our understanding of being part of God's family.

Alternatively, if we do not pray, we can miss these benefits and stray off into vindictive or self-centered behavior that corrodes our confession and our credibility. Refusing to pray reflects a rebellious spirit of independence that starts to separate us from God. Then, as we feel more and more like we are on our own, our pride may come into play to keep us headed in that direction. Like a sheep straying away from the flock and away from the Shepherd, we become more vulnerable to attack—a dangerous situation, and one to avoid!

Self-Examination

In addition to prayer, our response must include honest self-examination, clear-eyed introspection, and repentance. This is in no way meant to discount the possibility of hostility or persecution, but to check whether we have done something that deserves punishment and are mistaking the punishment for persecution. Thus, we stress words like "honest" and "clear-eyed" because, as Jeremiah 17:9–10 reminds us, "the heart is deceitful above all things" and we need to ask God to search our heart and mind for sin. We can be quite clever at explaining away our own behavior, so we need God's Word to cut through the rationalizations and show us the truth. Did we do something that actually deserves punishment under the law and yet try to claim to be victims of unfair hostility? If so, then we need God's scrutiny and

---

15 Hebrews 11:10, 15–16 describes this transcending perspective: "For [Abraham] was looking forward to the city that has foundations, whose designer and builder is God. . . . If [the heroes of the faith] had been thinking of that land from which they had gone out, they would have had opportunity to return. But as it is, they desire a better country, that is, a heavenly one. Therefore God is not ashamed to be called their God, for He has prepared for them a city."

we need to repent. Just punishment under God's Law or under the just laws of God-given government should not be waved off and mislabeled as hostility toward Christ or Christians.

Scripture is clear that we should not complain if we suffer for doing wrong. In fact, we should expect to be punished if we are in the wrong. Romans 13:3–4 says,

> For rulers are not a terror to good conduct, but to bad. Would you have no fear of the one who is in authority? Then do what is good, and you will receive his approval, for he is God's servant for your good. But if you do wrong, be afraid, for he does not bear the sword in vain. For he is the servant of God, an avenger who carries out God's wrath on the wrongdoer.

In other words, government is supposed to enforce God's justice in keeping with His definition of right and wrong.

If government has strayed from this purpose and we must choose between obeying God or governing authorities, then like Peter said in Acts 5:29, "we must obey God rather than men." Of course, Peter's situation was rather black and white: the religious and cultural rulers had ordered him not to speak of Christ or teach in His name. The situations we face may not be as clear-cut. For example, cultural and political forces in the United States are attempting to silence Christians who do not support homosexual marriage and are attempting to force business owners to support homosexual marriage against their religious convictions.[16] Although on the surface the issues seem clear, underlying questions arise that need both public scrutiny and personal self-examination. We Christians need to know whether we should submit to the cultural pressures, fight for our rights, or take some other course of action (these options come up for discussion in the next chapter). However, we also need to understand why to take one option over another, and this is where self-examination becomes necessary. Given the complexity of the challenges, we should also seek advice from our pastor, an

---

16 See, for example, Emily Belz, "A clerk's struggle," *WORLD News Group*, April 18, 2015; D. C. Innes, "The Christian baker's conscience," *WORLD News Group*, April 6, 2015; and Daniel James Devine, "Indiana governor signs RFRA 'fix,'" *WORLD News Group*, April 2, 2015.

elder or teacher, or a spiritually wise brother or sister in Christ as a reality check on our own understanding.

On the other hand, if the government is correct in its enforcement, we must heed 1 Peter 4:14–15, which says, "If you are insulted for the name of Christ, you are blessed, because the Spirit of glory and of God rests upon you. But let none of you suffer as a murderer or a thief or an evildoer or as a meddler." A meddler? That sets a pretty high bar for our behavior; which of us has not "meddled" at one time or another? In other words, we need to be squeaky-clean when it comes to whether our suffering is because of the name of Christ or because of us. Further, Peter's statement carries a promise: if we suffer unjustly as Christians, we are blessed and the Spirit rests upon us. What does the Spirit do? He comforts us and works to accomplish the Father's plans. The statement also suggests a serious implication: if we suffer because of our own wrongdoing, we are more likely to damage our credibility as Christians and bring dishonor to our Lord's name than to enjoy God's blessed approval.

So how do we examine ourselves, and against what kind of standard? Here is where a practical working familiarity with God's Law becomes essential. The Ten Commandments (Exodus 20:1–17) provide our starting point, but Jesus clarified for us their focus on God and on our neighbor when He was asked which is the greatest commandment. In Matthew 22:37–40, He answered, "You shall love the Lord your God with all your heart and with all your soul and with all your mind. This is the great and first commandment. And a second is like it: You shall love your neighbor as yourself. On these two commandments depend all the Law and the Prophets." We may have trouble seeing how these broad, deep commandments apply to our particular behavior or situation. If so, then we need to pray for God to enlighten us as to the true nature of our problem. He may do this through our study of the Bible, or He may speak to us through the insights of our pastor, an elder or teacher, or a spiritually wise brother or sister in Christ. Then, as we begin to understand the problem and our role in it, we need to confess, repent, and seek God's direction for what our changed behavior should look like. Note that if many of us (e.g., an entire community) are together in being at fault, it is important for each of us to follow the Lord rather than the group, particularly if the group sees no need to repent.

Finally, keep in mind that self-examination can run into problems in two ways. First, as mentioned before, we may have trouble being completely truthful with ourselves. In other words, our self-evaluation may not be honest. To avoid deceiving ourselves, we should seek advice from a mature Christian or our pastor, who can bring an independent or at least a less biased view to the question. Second, we may not be able to move past our self-examination to see how God would like to use us. In other words, even with good intentions and a hunger for the truth, we may fall into a victim mentality and find ourselves immobilized. In either case, we need to follow through in self-examination and seek God's restoration to rescue us from deceit and selfishness.

Forgiveness

Christians experience and proclaim God's forgiveness, and we must not deny our role in receiving and sharing His forgiveness even when the situation around us has become hostile. Forgiveness is not easy under the best of circumstances, and it becomes well-nigh impossible in the midst of persecution. We cannot do it on our own, but it is God's power in and through us that enables us to forgive. By God's grace, our response to hostility or persecution should include forgiveness as we forgive those who oppose us.

What does forgiveness do for our persecutors and for us? It means releasing them of their guilt, but that release often does not mean that the consequences will go away. It means letting go of our own desire for revenge, but may not mean relief from pain. This can seem incomplete from a personal point of view, so why do we forgive? In short, we forgive because we follow the command and example of Jesus. Matthew 6:14–15 relates the command where, right after giving us the Lord's Prayer, Jesus says, "For if you forgive others their trespasses, your heavenly Father will also forgive you, but if you do not forgive others their trespasses, neither will your Father forgive your trespasses." His example came from the cross, where Jesus prayed for His persecutors, "Father, forgive them, for they know not what they do" (Luke 23:34).

Additional examples from Scripture include Joseph forgiving his brothers and Stephen forgiving his attackers. Recall that Joseph's brothers kidnapped him and sold him into slavery in Egypt, but many years later, after their father Jacob died, they repented and asked for Joseph's forgiveness. Genesis 50:17b–21 records the scene:

> [Joseph's brothers said,] "And now, please forgive the transgression of the servants of the God of your father." Joseph wept when they spoke to him. His brothers also came and fell down before him and said, "Behold, we are your servants." But Joseph said to them, "Do not fear, for am I in the place of God? As for you, you meant evil against me, but God meant it for good, to bring it about that many people should be kept alive, as they are today. So do not fear; I will provide for you and your little ones." Thus he comforted them and spoke kindly to them.

One of the first deacons of the Church, Stephen, followed his Lord's example and asked God to forgive his persecutors as they were stoning him. Acts 7:57–60 tells us,

> They cried out with a loud voice and stopped their ears and rushed together at him. Then they cast him out of the city and stoned him. And the witnesses laid down their garments at the feet of a young man named Saul. And as they were stoning Stephen, he called out, "Lord Jesus, receive my spirit." And falling to his knees he cried out with a loud voice, "Lord, do not hold this sin against them." And when he had said this, he fell asleep.

One cannot help but wonder how Jacob's brothers and Stephen's persecutors felt when they heard words of comfort and forgiveness. Jacob's brothers no doubt felt relief, perhaps mixed with surprise, and hopefully this turned their focus toward the sovereign Lord who had blessed and sustained them through Joseph. Sadly, Stephen's persecutors stopped their ears out of rage against Stephen and the Lord, but if others who saw these events were open to God's grace, they could not help but be affected by Stephen's words of forgiveness.

More recent examples of forgiveness include the Amish families who forgave the man who shot and killed their daughters.[17] In October 2006, a gunman entered an Amish schoolhouse in Pennsylvania, murdered five schoolgirls, and then committed suicide. During the chaos that followed and in the midst of their suffering, Amish community leaders visited the gunman's widow and parents. They did not diminish the magnitude of the sin, nor did they offer cheap grace, but they offered forgiveness. Amazed by such an uncommon thing, the news media reported this story worldwide. An even more recent example involved the martyrdom of Coptic Christians in Libya. After the event, families of the victims were vocal about their forgiveness for the persecutors and spoke of praying for their salvation in Jesus Christ. Again, reporters were amazed and the story went far and wide.[18] Some will dismiss these examples of forgiveness as a fluke or even as cases of insanity, much as Stephen's persecutors stopped their ears against the truth. Yet we can only wonder at how many openings these startling examples of forgiveness create for Christians to discuss the reality of sin, our need to forgive and to be forgiven, and the power of the Gospel of Jesus Christ.

If we don't forgive, we are in effect refusing to let go of our grief and suffering. This puts us at risk of carrying a grudge, becoming absorbed in self or revenge, and becoming a slave to our suffering. Refusing to forgive means not sharing God's grace even though He offers us that grace so freely and abundantly, and it casts a shadow over the Christian community. If we do forgive, we find freedom to rise above our suffering as we focus on Christ. The explicit difficulty of forgiving our oppressor highlights the powerful message of God's mercy, adds credibility to our Gospel witness, and commands the attention of those who see but have not experienced God's grace. The whole idea of forgiving as God has forgiven us may be a foreign concept to most of our neighbors. God's grace is such a radical,

> If we don't forgive, we are in effect refusing to let go of our grief and suffering. If we do forgive, we find freedom to rise above our suffering as we focus on Christ.

---

17 Kate Naseef, "How can the Amish forgive what seems unforgivable?" *USA Today*, October 1, 2007.

18 "Videos of Christians forgiving Islamic State go viral in the Arab world," www.sat7.org/news-item/5401, March 13, 2015.

unworldly, sometimes even scandalous idea that the press may report it as a newsworthy event. If we confess God as the source of our ability to forgive, it can spark people to take a new look at their own spiritual condition and look toward God for hope of salvation. Regardless of how we have been wronged, by God's grace we forgive our oppressor for his sake, for our own sake, and to model the behavior of Christ. It is fundamentally part of the Gospel God gives us and gives others through us.

Bearing Witness

This leads to the next part of our response: to bear witness to what we believe, even in the midst of persecution. As described earlier, God will use our situation for His glory and to speak to those around us. We are not able to do this from our own strength or will, but He can and will do this from His faithfulness and sovereignty. So this is not a call for acting triumphantly, which carries its own emphasis on self. Instead, our tasks are simply to stand firm, stay faithful to Him, and share God's grace as opportunities arise, just as Christ stood firm, stayed the course, and offered God's grace to those around Him. We need to leave the triumph to Him! There will be times when we do well just to survive and don't have a lot of energy left for much of anything else, which is why we must rely on God.

Stand firm, stay faithful to Him, and share God's grace as opportunities arise.

How do we go about bearing witness, and to whom do we bear witness? As Christians, what we say and do reflect on God and, more specifically, on Jesus Christ since we bear His name. When we bear witness, we provide evidence about God and His character and, more to the point, Jesus Christ and the Gospel. We might provide evidence through words of sharing or testimony or through actions that people can see. This might happen through each of us as individuals or through groups of believers (i.e., the Church).

Is witness something intentional, or does it just sort of happen? The short answer is yes. We may have opportunities to speak directly of God or to speak of how we handle hostility and why we handle it that way. On the other hand, even if we do not have a chance to speak to our opponents, allies, or neutral parties, people will usually have a chance to see what we do and what we choose not to do and then draw their own conclusions. Life is a contact sport, and we need to remember that if we are Christians, then it is a given that those we come into contact with will receive some kind of witness from us, limited though it may be, whether or not we intend it.

Witness happens through words that we share with others. With persecution and suffering explicitly in mind, Peter wrote,

> But even if you should suffer for righteousness' sake, you will be blessed. Have no fear of them, nor be troubled, but in your hearts honor Christ the Lord as holy, always being prepared to make a defense to anyone who asks you for a reason for the hope that is in you; yet do it with gentleness and respect, having a good conscience, so that, when you are slandered, those who revile your good behavior in Christ may be put to shame. (1 Peter 3:14–16)

Our defense, then, involves sharing the reason for our hope in Christ, which means speaking of Jesus. Such a witness comes about not by clever words, persuasive arguments, or defeating opponents in public debate but by our steady, simple confession of Jesus Christ. This draws a worthwhile contrast between our desire for peace and holiness and the desires of our accusers, but it also serves an even more valuable role by pointing persecutors to the One who can redeem them.

Witness also happens through what we do or choose not to do, as mentioned above. In this sense, and perhaps unexpectedly, it could be either active or passive. We may choose to forgive, or we may hold a grudge. We may support our brothers and sisters in Christ, or we may choose not to. We may follow God's lead, leaning on Him for guidance and strength, or we may try to go it alone and on our own terms. When we make mistakes or sin, we may acknowledge it and apologize, or we may stiffen our necks in pride. We may try to show God's love by serving or supporting our neighbors, or we may stay focused on self. Even our attitudes will cry out to those around us! Actions often speak more loudly than words, so what we do or do not do speaks volumes to those who see.

Speaking of mistakes, what if I am an imperfect witness, unsteady or inconsistent in how I handle hostility? My mistakes and shortcomings do not cancel out God's ability to use my weakness to demonstrate His grace. As Paul wrote in 2 Corinthians 12:8–10,

> Three times I pleaded with the Lord about this, that it should leave me. But He said to me, "My grace is sufficient for you, for My power is made perfect in weakness." Therefore I will boast all the more gladly of my weaknesses, so that the power of Christ may rest upon me. For the sake of Christ, then, I am content with weaknesses, insults, hardships, persecutions, and calamities. For when I am weak, then I am strong.

Further, recognizing that we must rely on God, it is the Holy Spirit who makes our witness effective and who will make our situation bear fruit for God's glory. It is our witness, but it is His power.

What makes our personal witness valuable or special? It could be a matter of being in the right place at the right time, which God will orchestrate. The twenty-one Christians martyred by ISIS in Libya early in 2015 refused to recant their faith and were heard praying to Jesus just before they died. This by itself was a profound, unplanned witness to glorify God, but the Holy Spirit has already been using it to touch hearts and minds.[19] Jesus was faithful to the point of death; we simply follow Him on the path He places before us.

It is our witness, but it is His power.

As it says in 1 Peter 2:21, "For to this you have been called, because Christ also suffered for you, leaving you an example, so that you might follow in His steps." Our task is to remain faithful, living and speaking God's truth, while the Holy Spirit plants, waters, and nurtures the seed of the Gospel.

Mutual Support

As we respond to hostility, we should take steps to provide mutual support to our brothers and sisters in the Christian community. As 1 Corinthians 12:26–27 explains, "If one member suffers, all suffer together; if one member is honored, all rejoice together. Now you are the body of

---

19   Jayson Casper, "How Libya's Martyrs Are Witnessing to Egypt," *Christianity Today*, February 23, 2015.

Christ and individually members of it." When another part of the Body of Christ suffers, we may have the opportunity and obligation to provide support or other tangible or intangible forms of encouragement. If we are the ones suffering, we should not stand on false humility but should allow other Christians to support us. To make a helpful start, think about what you would like your brothers and sisters in Christ to do in your support if you encounter persecution. Then think about how you might be able to support them if the tables were turned. Given a few minutes of reflection, you can probably come up with several ideas for how you could make a difference in the lives of the persecuted. And nongovernment organizations (NGOs), such as Christian Freedom International, In Defense of Christians, The Lutheran Church—Missouri Synod (and its service organizations), Open Doors USA, and Voice of the Martyrs (all listed in Appendix 1) can provide many additional ideas and venues for support.

Support might include words of encouragement to individuals, groups, or congregations, at least to the extent that freedom of speech and freedom of assembly exist, communications are intact between Christians, and the necessary relationships of trust are in place or can be developed. If nearby, we can support our brothers and sisters with encouraging words, prayers, personal friendship, physical contact (e.g., a hug, a handshake, or a look in the eye), listening, enduring together, or worshiping together. Material support might include assistance such as food, money, housing, transportation, medical care, assistance with property, or other necessities of life. Other forms of mutual support might include speaking out on one another's behalf, and of course it provides further opportunities to glorify God and profess our motivation and our faith to those around us. It may be more difficult to make a personal impact at a distance, but we can pray; send encouraging words, funding, or missionary or logistical support; or perhaps try to intervene through political or economic pressure or by public opinion.

Two examples of support come readily to mind from Scripture. First, consider how Paul counted on prayer support from the churches. Nearly every one of his letters includes a request that they pray for him, the ministry, and by implication, his survival through myriad unexpected difficulties. For example, Ephesians 6:18b–20 says, "Keep alert with all perseverance, making supplication for all the saints, and also for me, that words may be given to me in opening my mouth boldly to proclaim the mystery of the

Gospel, for which I am an ambassador in chains, that I may declare it boldly, as I ought to speak." Notice that Paul does not request prayer for his release from suffering, but requests prayer for the effectiveness of his witness.

Second, consider how individuals and congregations provided material support, fellowship, and refreshment or encouragement. For example, in 2 Timothy 1:16–18, Paul writes,

> May the Lord grant mercy to the household of Onesiphorus, for he often refreshed me and was not ashamed of my chains, but when he arrived in Rome he searched for me earnestly and found me—may the Lord grant him to find mercy from the Lord on that Day!—and you well know all the service he rendered at Ephesus.

In 2 Corinthians 8:1–5, Paul shows us a compelling example of material support as he writes,

> We want you to know, brothers, about the grace of God that has been given among the churches of Macedonia, for in a severe test of affliction, their abundance of joy and their extreme poverty have overflowed in a wealth of generosity on their part. For they gave according to their means, as I can testify, and beyond their means, of their own accord, begging us earnestly for the favor of taking part in the relief of the saints—and this, not as we expected, but they gave themselves first to the Lord and then by the will of God to us.

Healthy fellowship within or between congregations is a good indicator of how mutual support can develop and bear fruit. The examples mentioned above from Paul's epistles provide illustrations of how congregations could, with God's help, rise above their limitations and look beyond their self-interests to support the Body of Christ. In contrast, an unhealthy fellowship models how support can fall short or even fall victim to selfish behavior. Mutual support, done in the name of Christ, is a form of witness in itself. It is also valuable in enabling the suffering Christians to survive, persevere, and carry on. On the other hand, lack of support makes us look like any other non-Christian group of people. While it also may pull the rug out from under those who are suffering, God may raise up help from a different direction, to our shame and to their credit.

There are at least two reasons why relationships of trust are part of this discussion. First, we would like to be assured that any investment of time, energy, or other resources represents good stewardship and that it is not wasted. In cases where it may not be possible to have this assurance, it is probably better to err on the side of generosity than to risk leaving fellow Christians without support. Trust is a helpful part of knowing that we are doing the right thing. Second, relationships of trust come up because there are some people and groups that cannot be trusted with confidential information or certain kinds of support. A corrupt government, for example, may pocket any resources that we attempt to send to the oppressed, and in some cases the persecutors may try to intercept our communications to identify new targets for hostility. So caution is in order not only for the sake of good stewardship, but also in an attempt to avoid doing inadvertent harm.

Another dimension of support involves being prepared to speak the truth in love, and it is important to note that this might require sharing Law, Gospel, or both as appropriate. It also involves pastoral support and counseling and brotherly hand-on-the-shoulder encouragement and exhortation. We are often good at speaking truth without adequate sympathetic support, and we are often good at sympathetic support while minimizing the truth. To provide complete, holistic support we need truth and love, mind and heart, to minister to the whole person. And as we minister to one another, we need to point the other person to Jesus Christ, who alone can sustain us with strength and real, lasting peace.

Before moving on to the next topic, we need to be realistic and acknowledge that under the stress of hostility or persecution, the unity of our Christian fellowship may start to fray. There may be legitimate differences of opinion about how to respond to the situation, and some of our friends may start to buckle under the pressure. To the extent possible, we need to maintain the unity of the fellowship since that directly impacts the credibility of our identity in Christ.[20] However, some of us may still disagree

---

20 In John 13:34–35, Jesus declares, "A new commandment I give to you, that you love one another:

on how to respond to the hostility or persecution. If so, then perhaps we need to love one another, agree to disagree, and avoid doing anything that would undercut our brothers and sisters in Christ. What if one of our fellow Christians folds under the duress and denies the faith? We cannot really know what happened unless we are there to witness the event, and we cannot see what is in that person's heart either at that time or later. Recall from our earlier discussion that Satan demanded permission to sift Peter; Peter denied knowing Christ, apparently under Satan's attack; and yet Jesus reinstated Peter, knowing that (as He had prayed) Peter's faith had not failed. Rather than judging or condemning our broken brother, we should offer them God's grace and seek a restored fellowship based on God's Word. Put another way, if they welcome God's grace and seek to rejoin the Church and continue in His Word, then we welcome them back. If they turn their back on God's Word and go in a different direction, then we may have no choice but to let them go. And this leads to our next spiritual discipline: knowing what we believe.

Knowing What We Believe

Finally, it should probably go without saying, but we will say it anyway: when you face hostility or persecution, you need to know what you believe. This spiritual discipline involves being immersed in God's Word. It also requires the stabilizing influence of the Christian Church, which can help us avoid veering off into our own understanding in a way that turns aside from the historic, orthodox, confessional understanding of God's truth. We learn and understand what we believe from personal and group Bible study and from our pastors, teachers, study leaders, and spiritually mature fellow Christians, all empowered by the Holy Spirit to share with us the Word of God. Hebrews 4:12 describes this Word as "living and active, sharper than any two-edged sword, piercing to the division of soul and of spirit, of joints and of marrow, and discerning the thoughts and intentions of the heart." Knowing what we believe involves head knowledge and understanding in our heart.

---

just as I have loved you, you also are to love one another. By this all people will know that you are My disciples, if you have love for one another." By this commandment Jesus is staking our identity as His disciples on how we treat one another.

As we encounter hostility and persecution, we will also encounter competing spiritual, religious, or values-laden claims; false teaching; distorted truth; or expediency-based interpretations of Scripture. Each of these will attempt to separate us from God's truth, and we can expect those who oppose or persecute us to have their own version of truth. They may be completely ignorant of God's truth, contemptuous of God and His Word, or even practice a well-oiled, salvation-by-self variation of the Gospel. Some of what we encounter will be well meaning but simply wrong; some will be driven by secular or multicultural or religious worldviews or simply by non-Christian belief systems; and some may even be demonic. Whether overt or covert, the forces that try to move us away from God's truth will usually combine some mix of truth and error in a deceptive, appealing combination. And it might combine persuasion with coercion. After all, the evil one sometimes appears as an angel of light[21] and is also known as the father of lies.[22]

We need to stick to God's truth in general, and to the Gospel of Jesus Christ in particular, or we lose our bearings, and our spiritual health and welfare are at risk. This is of much greater consequence than our physical health. But when persuasion and coercion arrive part and parcel with the hostility, how can we know what is false to be able to resist it? Counterfeits come in many shapes and forms, so the best way to spot a counterfeit is to know the genuine article so well that we can immediately spot anything that is different. So, we need to know the truth, and we need to know what we believe. Linking back to our earlier discussion of mutual support, we also need a circle of fellow believers who can encourage us and hold us accountable to that truth, and who can help spot the flaws in the arguments and rationalizations of those who oppose us.

Recall from our earlier discussion that roots of hostility include original sin, opposition to Christ, and spiritual warfare. Ephesians 6:12 notes, "For we do not wrestle against flesh and blood, but against the rulers, against the authorities, against the cosmic powers over this present darkness, against the spiritual forces of evil in the heavenly places." In addition, 1 Peter 5:8

---

21 "Even Satan disguises himself as an angel of light. So it is no surprise if his servants, also, disguise themselves as servants of righteousness" (2 Corinthians 11:14–15).

22 In John 8:44, Jesus warns, "[The devil] was a murderer from the beginning, and does not stand in the truth, because there is no truth in him. When he lies, he speaks out of his own character, for he is a liar and the father of lies."

reminds us that "[our] adversary the devil prowls around like a roaring lion, seeking someone to devour." We may not ever see the full picture when it comes to spiritual warfare since so much of it apparently happens beyond the reach of our senses, but we need to be aware of some of the evil one's favorite tactics. These include falsehood, as described above, but they also include discouragement, confusion, isolation or separation from Christian fellowship, division in the Church, or some other kind of attack. Many or all of these can involve falsehood since, for example, a false perception of isolation can be just as effective as real isolation.

Knowing what we believe (i.e., knowing God's truth) is crucial to discerning and surviving spiritual attacks, regardless of whether the attacks take on physical or emotional attributes. Again looking to Scripture, Ephesians 6:13–18 admonishes,

> Take up the whole armor of God, that you may be able to withstand in the evil day, and having done all, to stand firm. Stand therefore, having fastened on the belt of truth, and having put on the breastplate of righteousness, and, as shoes for your feet, having put on the readiness given by the Gospel of peace. In all circumstances take up the shield of faith, with which you can extinguish all the flaming darts of the evil one; and take the helmet of salvation, and the sword of the Spirit, which is the word of God, praying at all times in the Spirit, with all prayer and supplication. To that end keep alert with all perseverance, making supplication for all the saints.

And may our prayers for one another be persistent!

⌘⌘

Discussion Questions

1. Have you ever felt your job was at risk or you were threatened in some way because of your faith in Christ? Explain.

2. Consider the spiritual disciplines we discussed in this chapter. Which one is your strongest and which is your weakest? How could you become stronger in this area?

3. What do you need to pray in the event of hostility or persecution against you or others?

4. Why is it hard to forgive our enemies? What could God do to make it easier for you?

5. What kind of support from other Christians might you like to have if you faced serious opposition or persecution for your faith?

5

Christian Response: Options for Action

With time and experience, we will find that the spiritual disciplines described in the previous chapter are appropriate to essentially every situation of hostility, oppression, or persecution we encounter. However, each situation is different and dynamic, and circumstances change with time. Our opponents and persecutors are likely to change their behavior, either to continue their attack or to break it off. And, of course, God is sovereign and sees our plight and may intervene in ways that we might or might not understand.

In addition to the common themes represented by the spiritual disciplines, the Bible gives us several options that we might be able to choose from in responding to our situation. Scripture presents some of these options in clear statements of direction and other options by examples of God working in the lives of His saints. Some of them we can infer from what Jesus taught and from what we know of God's concerns and priorities. Here is a simple example: 1 Timothy 2:4 tells us that God "desires all people to be saved and to come to the knowledge of the truth." This desire of God should inform our response to persecution. Given a choice between actions that would remove proclamation of the Gospel from where we are and actions that would allow sharing the Gospel to continue, and other factors being equal, we should lean toward the latter set of options. This chapter aims to outline and explain several different options for our responses, and the chapter that follows will look into how we decide what to do. But first we need to look at the difference between reacting and responding.

Even if by God's grace we grow in the spiritual disciplines, we still need to face the inconsistency of our discipleship and our tendency to react rather than respond to hostility. Reacting implies that we are self-interested and driven by events, while responding implies that we are intentional, deliberate, and, hopefully, living by the heart and mind of Christ rather than self. God can use the situation for His purposes in either case, but while reacting may put us at cross-purposes with His will, responding involves yielding to His desire to guide our behavior.

We are, however, sinners—weak and subject to mistakes and lapses in judgment. In fact, our first reaction to hostility might often involve defensive attitudes and behavior. Although we would like to believe that we are defending the truth, as we continue to react, we could get into arguments and risk coming across as mean-spirited and selfish. In this kind of situation, it is all too easy to damage both our credibility and our opportunity to speak of God. Defensive behavior can be offensive to those around us! If we fall into this trap, then we need to admit that our behavior is defensive and ultimately self-centered, rather than Christlike. We need to repent and get past this before we can move forward in a constructive way.

So how do we avoid the trap of defensive behavior? First, we need to return to spiritual disciplines such as self-examination, prayer, and repentance—all rooted in God's grace. We need to remember that this is not about us but about how God would use us in a given situation. Then, with God's strength and guidance, we need to take a clear-eyed look at our circumstances and choices. If events are moving too quickly for us to respond in an intentional way, then that is all the more reason to prepare beforehand by being firmly grounded in God's Word and spiritual disciplines. Navigating a canoe through whitewater rapids provides an apt analogy.

If you paddle a canoe down a wild river, you have a choice to make when you reach a stretch of rapids. You can simply go with the flow, ride the current through the rough patch, and take your chances on whether you will hit a rock and crash. Or you can stop, take stock of what lies ahead, and make an informed decision about how to navigate the rapids. You may not ever have as much information as you would like, you may encounter a surprise or two along the way, and you may even still hit a rock. But the odds of disaster are much greater if you simply paddle ahead, expecting to always be able to react to events in the right way and at the right time. You will have a much better chance at success if you take a disciplined approach.

As we rely on God rather than self, we have the resources we need when we need them. After all, in the Great Commission our Lord promised to be with us to the end of the age! For the sake of our credibility and Gospel witness, we must focus on God rather than self as we discern His path forward through the rapids. This leads to several possible courses of action, which we will discuss in the sections that follow.

Turn the Other Cheek

The first alternatives that come to mind when we encounter hostility are often to turn the other cheek or go the extra mile. In the Sermon on the Mount, our Lord said,

> You have heard that it was said, "An eye for an eye and a tooth for a tooth." But I say to you, do not resist the one who is evil. But if anyone slaps you on the right cheek, turn to him the other also. And if anyone would sue you and take your tunic, let him have your cloak as well. And if anyone forces you to go one mile, go with him two miles. (Matthew 5:38–41)

Turning the other cheek implies submitting to harsh treatment, often in ways that are clearly unreasonable and unjust. However, taking these two commands by themselves without the "eye for an eye" statement that precedes them robs them of some important context.

This is one of several passages in the Sermon on the Mount in which Jesus starts with a part of the Law ("You have heard it said . . . ") that we sinners are inclined to distort, and then describes the behavior ("but I say to you . . .") that He desires instead. To understand the desired behaviors, then, we must look at the distorted behaviors they aim to replace. In this case, the eye-for-an-eye concept had come to mean a demand for vengeance that crowded out mercy and inserted self-interest in place of justice provided by government or God. Jesus' words point us in the direction of humility and faith, away from arrogance and self-righteousness. With this in mind, turning the other cheek to those opposing us is part of a winsome, active behavior that gains a hearing for the Gospel and allows us opportunities to show God's grace. This may require time, money, material goods (e.g., giving up our cloak), or other kinds of effort on our part.

In the extreme, God may call us to mimic Christ, who gave up His glory to be born here as a baby, lived in His creation, submitted to the governing authorities, and ultimately yielded His life. We may not have to die for it (or we might!), but this behavior actualizes Jesus' admonition about giving up our life to gain life that matters, instead of gaining this life only to lose the life that matters. He explained this in Matthew 16:24–26, where He said,

> If anyone would come after Me, let him deny himself and take up his cross and follow Me. For whoever would save his life will lose it, but whoever loses his life for My sake will find it. For what will it profit a man if he gains the whole world and forfeits his soul? Or what shall a man give in return for his soul?

Actions are crucial when we consider these options, but so is our attitude. It is hard to turn the cheek or go the extra mile without resentment, anger, or some degree of bitterness, and a bitter attitude can wipe out any opportunity we have to speak of God's love. Turning the cheek or going the extra mile implies some degree of self-sacrifice, since in some cases we may have no choice in the matter, while in other cases we willingly submit even though we did not have to submit. Regardless, in addition to submitting to those who make a demand of us, perhaps out of hostility or as part of their persecution of us, we must also find a way to make our feelings submit. Submitting, even though unfairly treated, was exactly what Christ did, and our submitting may be key to pointing people to Him.

In the Sermon on the Mount, our Lord teaches that sinful feelings (e.g., lust or anger) are just as dangerous as sinful actions (e.g., adultery or murder). This is a difficult standard to expect us to reach, so we have no choice but to depend on God's grace and on Jesus to fulfill the expectation for us. This leads to the idea that we must force our will, feelings, and behavior into submission. As Paul explained, "Every athlete exercises self-control in all things. They do it to receive a perishable wreath, but we an imperishable. So I do not run aimlessly; I do not box as one beating the air. But I discipline my body and keep it under control, lest after preaching to others I myself should be disqualified" (1 Corinthians 9:25–27). Otherwise, we fall short and risk bringing God's grace and Jesus' fulfillment of the Law on our behalf into disrepute.

Turning the cheek to a hostile person, going the extra mile to carry a soldier's burden, or giving up a cloak were all obvious examples from centuries past. Typically, these were one-of-a-kind events rather than something that happened every day. What might this action look like today? Examples from current events might include bakers or florists who willingly choose to serve homosexual couples or other customers whose behavior flagrantly violates God's laws. A less controversial but still significant example might be a university Christian group who willingly moves off campus to comply with rules that discriminate against Christians. Public examples are not easy to locate, though, because this kind of Christlike behavior often goes unnoticed by the news media and perhaps even by the Church at large.

On a more personal level, how do we handle insulting comments, misrepresentations, or slander that might come our way because of our faith? We could push back or argue the point, but that might have the perverse effect of lending credibility to those who oppose us, since, by our actions, we suggest that their point is worth arguing. For example, 2 Timothy 2:23 says, "Have nothing to do with foolish, ignorant controversies; you know that they breed quarrels." On the other hand, while we could certainly just smile and go our way, sometimes we need to speak the truth or else the false accusations might be allowed to stand uncontested. We need to discern what kind of response is most appropriate for the situation, and sometimes the best approach is to turn the other cheek by remaining silent, staying our course, and expecting that truth will win out and that God will redeem the situation in His own time.[1]

---

1   See Marvin Olasky, "Half-baked reporting," *WORLD News Group*, February 6, 2015, for a recent example.

Positive aspects of turning the other cheek are also situational. They might include self-discipline and personal growth, winning credibility or sympathy from persecutors or observers (particularly if this enhances our witness to the Gospel), exposing hostility for others to see, and perhaps deflecting hostility toward us and away from other Christians who are less able to bear it. A recent, partial example might be the variety of reactions among people in Egypt when they learned that Egyptian Christians captured by ISIS (Muslim extremists) had been executed in Libya.[2] This situation is still in flux, but we can see at least some of the positive effects in play. In other cases, the impacts of us turning the other cheek may not take place in a time or place that we can see, but that should not deter us from following our Lord in this behavior.

The downsides of not turning the other cheek, or of first turning the other cheek and then changing course, are also situational. They include the possibility of appearing selfish, accusations of hypocrisy or hostility (e.g., being accused of hate speech or bigotry for simply speaking the truth) by those who would oppose us, and lost opportunities for serving or witnessing. This means that we need to consider not only our options for responding to hostility but also the implications of different courses of action and possible consequences if we do not follow through in good faith. Ultimately, our choices are not about us as much as they are about the Gospel.

Invoke Our Rights

A second option for responding to hostility involves invoking our rights as citizens, particularly if we can use our citizenship to serve the Gospel. This option may not be mutually exclusive with turning the other cheek or with some of the other options. It is important to note that this involves claiming rights that our neighbors would recognize rather than claiming any special status as a Christian or inventing rights on our own.

Paul invoked his Roman citizenship when facing hostility on at least three different occasions: (1) Acts 16:37–39a relates,

---

2   Jayson Casper, "Libya's 21 Christian Martyrs: 'With Their Blood, They Are Unifying Egypt,'" *Christianity Today*, February 18, 2015; and Jayson Casper, "How Libya's Martyrs Are Witnessing to Egypt," *Christianity Today*, February 23, 2015.

But Paul said to them [the police], "They have beaten us publicly, uncondemned, men who are Roman citizens, and have thrown us into prison; and do they now throw us out secretly? No! Let them come themselves and take us out." The police reported these words to the magistrates, and they were afraid when they heard that they were Roman citizens. So they came and apologized to them.

(2) Acts 22:25–29 records,

But when they had stretched him out for the whips, Paul said to the centurion who was standing by, "Is it lawful for you to flog a man who is a Roman citizen and uncondemned?" When the centurion heard this, he went to the tribune and said to him, "What are you about to do? For this man is a Roman citizen." So the tribune came and said to him, "Tell me, are you a Roman citizen?" And he said, "Yes." The tribune answered, "I bought this citizenship for a large sum." Paul said, "But I am a citizen by birth." So those who were about to examine him withdrew from him immediately, and the tribune also was afraid, for he realized that Paul was a Roman citizen and that he had bound him.

And (3) Acts 25:10–12 says,

But Paul said, "I am standing before Caesar's tribunal, where I ought to be tried. To the Jews I have done no wrong, as you yourself know very well. If then I am a wrongdoer and have committed anything for which I deserve to die, I do not seek to escape death. But if there is nothing to their charges against me, no one can give me up to them. I appeal to Caesar." Then Festus, when he had conferred with his council, answered, "To Caesar you have appealed; to Caesar you shall go."

The rights Paul claimed at various times under the laws of Rome included the right to legal process, the right to a trial, the right to appeal a trial's outcome, the right to protection from unlawful imprisonment, and the right to physical protection from attack. But why would Paul invoke his rights? To preserve or obtain opportunities to speak the Gospel! Indirectly, he also forced the authorities to recognize the legitimacy of local Christian congregations (because they included citizens of Rome) rather than simply writing them off as one more group of troublesome outsiders. By invoking his citizenship, Paul also had the chance to take the Gospel to the capital of the Roman Empire, and with an armed escort to protect him on the journey.

Just as Paul had rights as a citizen of Rome that citizens of other countries did not have, rights of citizens today vary by country according to the type of governance under which they live. Our rights in the United States are more wide-ranging than those of ancient Rome, allowing for a lot of flexibility in application. The U.S. and state constitutions, including the Bill of Rights, civil law, and judicial decisions that interpret the law, all combine to define our rights as U.S. citizens. Since the U.S. and state governments are all representative democracies, we voters are eventually (if not immediately) responsible for the governance that protects our rights.[3] The situation is dynamic, though, in the sense that judicial decisions or legislative activity can change our rights, sometimes in substantial or unforeseen ways. Under federal and state constitutions and the evolving body of law, and of course depending on circumstances, our rights as citizens include these:

- Freedom of speech, freedom of assembly, and freedom of religion, all of which are valuable for unfettered proclamation of the Gospel and service in God's kingdom—this is not necessary for what Luther called God's kingdom of the right hand,[4] the heavenly kingdom where He rules directly, but it certainly makes our life easier.

- Freedom of speech and freedom of assembly to participate in our local community in an honest attempt to influence

---

3   The Commission on Theology and Church Relations report *Render Unto Caesar . . . and Unto God: A Lutheran View of Church and State* (St. Louis: The Lutheran Church—Missouri Synod, 1996) discusses many important aspects of the rights and responsibilities of Christians as citizens of the state.

4   This is a good place to remember Luther's concept of the kingdoms of the left hand and right hand and to remember that we hold dual citizenship: we are citizens of heaven and members of the family of God, even while we are still living here on earth as citizens of one nation or another. The nations (and citizenship) of this world are temporal while our citizenship in heaven is eternal, and the authority of governments of this world is subservient to the ultimate sovereignty of God.

community opinion, social values, and policy decisions as people influence their elected officials—this is part of what Luther called God's kingdom of the left hand, where God rules through civil government.

- Voting, petitioning the government, serving on juries, and running for public office, which provide ways for us to participate in governing and judicial processes at federal, state, and local levels.

- Seeking protection or relief in the courts through lawsuits, injunctions, due process, and trial by a jury of peers, which can provide tools to seek court protection against hostility or some of its effects that would block the Gospel.

- Conscientious objector status, which supports our right to obey God rather than men.

- Self-defense, which normally means protecting ourselves against physical harm, but not necessarily a right to protect property.

Invoking our rights as citizens involves first understanding specifically what rights we have, because they actually differ from country to country and perhaps from state to state in the U.S., and they may change over time as governing laws change. Once we understand what rights we have as citizens, we need to evaluate our situation to know what relevant options we might have under the law. This implies that we need to understand our rights well enough to know how they might apply on the fly, or in real time, or else we need to know whom we can go to for legal advice. Practically speaking, we probably need some degree of personal knowledge of the cognizant laws and we may need legal counsel to make the best use of some of our rights.

As citizens and voters, we need to exercise and guard our rights or they may be eroded with time. For example, over the past few years, members of the executive branch of the federal government have chosen to speak of one of the rights found under the First Amendment to the U.S. Constitution as a right of freedom of worship, deliberately avoiding the phrase "freedom of religion." If left unchecked, this would lead to restrictions on practicing religion outside the walls of the church. Fortunately, this potential infringe-ment on our rights has been noticed in the context of limits on ministry outside of worship services (e.g., freedom to speak of abortion and its effects in our communities) and is being fought successfully through the courts. Similarly, the June 2015 U.S. Supreme Court decision to legalize same-sex marriage across the nation touched off wide-ranging questions about how this decision might impact religious freedom and other constitutional and civic rights.[5] Answers to these questions will no doubt evolve over time in subsequent court cases, legal decisions, and legislation. In both examples, though, the warning is clear: we need to be on our guard.

Other more specific current examples of invoking our rights as citizens include the use of legal action to seek protection from government infringe-ment on freedom of religion, seeking legal protection for freedom of speech, and engaging the political process to seek or protect freedom of religion. In the first example, dozens of organizations (many, but not all, are Chris-tian) have taken legal action to prevent the U.S. government from using the Affordable Care Act to force them to pay for chemically induced abortions.[6] The second example involves government attempts to intimidate pastors in Texas because the pastors were using their right of free speech to speak out about preferential treatment for homosexuals.[7] In the third example, from India, citizens and politicians are using a political process in an attempt to influence laws that regulate conversions from one religion to another.[8]

As a rule, we seek options that align with God's will, and this will affect our choices for action. First Timothy 2:1–4 says,

---

5   Tamara Audi and Jacob Gershman, "Religious Groups Vow to Fight Gay Marriage Despite Su-preme Court," *The Wall Street Journal*, June 26, 2015 and Marvin Olasky, "Warnings from the Supreme Court," *WORLD News Group*, June 26, 2015.

6   Lawsuits have been filed against the U.S. government by at least twenty organizations ranging from Wheaton College to the University of Notre Dame to the Hobby Lobby chain of stores, and these have been widely reported in the news media. See, for example, D. C. Innes, "The fight for religious liberty," *WORLD News Group*, January 26, 2015, for a short, general discussion with links to other references.

7   Andrew Branch, "City demands pastors' sermons in LGBT lawsuit," *WORLD News Group*, October 15, 2014.

8   See Shanoor Seervai, "The Arguments For and Against a National Anti-Conversion Law," *The Wall Street Journal*, January 9, 2015; and Julia A. Seymour, "Christians demand Modi take a stand in India's conversion debate," *WORLD News Group*, January 12, 2015.

> First of all, then, I urge that supplications, prayers, intercessions, and thanksgivings be made for all people, for kings and all who are in high positions, that we may lead a peaceful and quiet life, godly and dignified in every way. This is good, and it is pleasing in the sight of God our Savior, who desires all people to be saved and to come to the knowledge of the truth.

This passage informs our choices in two ways. First, it is clear that we live under the rule of those who are in "high positions." In turn, those people are subordinate to God (whether or not they realize it) or we would not be praying to God on their behalf. So God, rather than worldly civil structure, is our ultimate authority. Second, our ultimate sovereign, God, desires for all to be saved and to come to the knowledge of the truth. This is not just any truth, but His truth, the Gospel. Therefore, strange as it may seem, there may be times when we choose to refrain from self-defense or decline government protection because we want complete freedom to speak and act without waiting on the civil authorities, or perhaps even without their awareness. We must keep the cross of Christ in mind and seek His guidance to recognize these situations and discern what to do.

Advantages of invoking our civil rights include protecting the public proclamation of the Gospel as well as our freedom to congregate, worship, serve, and minister as we see fit—these are worth fighting for! More broadly, this guards our right to believe and live according to God's Word and our right to speak the truth in love by sharing Law and Gospel where the competition of ideas and worldviews is in progress, in the public square. "Public square" might include colleges and universities, government organizations and processes, and community venues.

Potential problems arise when Christians are seen as whiners or as bullies, though such charges may often be false and need to be contested, which in turn requires freedom to do so.[9] Another potential downside could be the temptation to rely on civic rights while forgetting God's guidance, authority, and protection, or even for the church to veer off into becoming too political.[10] However, unless we are ready to accept government trying to assume

---

9   For an example of one such battle still in progress, see Daniel James Devine, "Indiana governor signs RFRA 'fix,'" *WORLD News Group*, April 2, 2015.

10   The Commission on Theology and Church Relations report *Render Unto Caesar . . . and Unto God*

God's role of guiding us on questions of what is true, appropriate, or fair, we need to stay alert and be ready to exercise our rights for the good of our country and even more so for the sake of the Gospel.

Disengage

A third practical alternative could be to disengage from the situation, which could involve going underground ("under the radar" or "off the grid") or perhaps taking the Gospel elsewhere. This might mean withdrawal or withholding of God's Word from those who despise and reject it, rather than withdrawing all Christian presence per se, or it might mean redirecting our ministry to where people are willing to receive it. Either way, we would curtail our dialogue and interaction with enemies of the Gospel, reduce our public presence, and reinvest the time and energy with people in the same community or nearby who are willing to listen and consider God's Word. Perhaps with this in mind, Jesus told His disciples, "Do not give dogs what is holy, and do not throw your pearls before pigs, lest they trample them underfoot and turn to attack you" (Matthew 7:6). In the context of that time, dogs were vicious animals that were often unclean, and pigs were unclean and could be vicious as well. Dogs and pigs live from meal to meal, with selfish interest being their primary concern.[11] The warning about trampling the pearls and attacking the person who brought them suggests that we need to be able to discern when it might be time to disengage and step away from trouble, both for the sake of the Gospel and for our sake as well. While such a step may look unfortunate according to our perspective, it might mean withdrawing from the public square while controversies sort themselves out or while we wait for God to correct the situation. Disengaging might look like a temporary change or a permanent one, depending on how the situation evolves, but even if it looks permanent to us it is still temporary on God's time scale.

---

examines some of the risks of the church becoming too political as well as the risks of the church ignoring the public square.

11 This calls to mind Philippians 3:18–19, which says, "For many, of whom I have often told you and now tell you even with tears, walk as enemies of the cross of Christ. Their end is destruction, their god is their belly, and they glory in their shame, with minds set on earthly things." Could Paul have been thinking about dogs, pigs, and the words of Christ when he wrote this?

Our feelings about having to step back and refocus may be similar to those of the Old Testament prophets as they spoke God's Word to Israel and were met with a frustrating level of indifference and hostility. Habakkuk 1:2–4, for example, relates the prophet's frustrations as he waited for God's justice in Israel:

> O Lord, how long shall I cry for help, and You will not hear? Or cry to You "Violence!" and You will not save? Why do You make me see iniquity, and why do You idly look at wrong? Destruction and violence are before me; strife and contention arise. So the law is paralyzed, and justice never goes forth. For the wicked surround the righteous; so justice goes forth perverted.

God replied to Habakkuk in the very next verse, "Look among the nations, and see; wonder and be astounded. For I am doing a work in your days that you would not believe if told" (v. 5). God said "in your days," yet it is important to see that God corrected matters on His schedule and not on Habakkuk's. Likewise, God will correct the situation around us on His schedule and will do so to achieve His goals rather than working to our personal satisfaction. Further, some elements of God's correction may not be immediately obvious. Elijah thought he was the last one in Israel who cared about the spiritual health of the nation, yet the remnant of seven thousand that God preserved in Israel (1 Kings 19:18) during the reign of Ahaz and Jezebel may be examples of God's people staying out of sight and out of mind while He worked to revitalize the nation.

In a different twist on this option, we may need to discern when to step back and chart a different course of action to avoid giving enemies of the cross an illegitimate credibility in the eyes of other people. Such credibility comes with time, attention, and debate from Christians; the fact that we push back on hostile arguments, and the way in which we push back, can sometimes give those hostile arguments credibility in the eyes of uninformed neutral observers. In those cases, continuing to share God's grace may invite higher levels of hostility and divert time and energy from sharing the Gospel where people are open to hearing it. Scripture also tells us to avoid close fellowship with false teachers, those who claim to be Christians but who teach false doctrine, mentioning specifically those who deny that Christ came in the flesh and those who do not abide in the teaching of Christ.[12] Note that these are fundamental issues rather than a dispute over styles of music, formality of worship, or similar adiaphora; the command involves whether an opponent who claims to be a Christian confesses the true nature of Jesus Christ, His work, and His Word. Thus, this command helps us avoid giving false Christians, who can be formidable opponents, an opening or a legitimacy that they do not deserve, particularly in the eyes of non-Christians who need to hear the true Gospel. Further, it helps us focus our ministry on those willing to receive it.

Did Paul ever withhold his preaching and teaching? Yes, there were times when he took the Gospel to the Jews, encountered opposition, and then withdrew and turned to the Gentiles in the same general area. We find one example in Acts 13:44–46:

> The next Sabbath almost the whole city gathered to hear the word of the Lord. But when the Jews saw the crowds, they were filled with jealousy and began to contradict what was spoken by Paul, reviling him. And Paul and Barnabas spoke out boldly, saying, "It was necessary that the word of God be spoken first to you. Since you thrust it aside and judge yourselves unworthy of eternal life, behold, we are turning to the Gentiles."

A second example turns up in Acts 14:5–7, which says, "When an attempt was made by both Gentiles and Jews, with their rulers, to mistreat them and to stone them, they learned of it and fled to Lystra and Derbe, cities of Lycaonia, and to the surrounding country, and there they continued to preach the gospel."

What might this option of disengagement look like today? If we disengage by going underground, then almost by definition there is not much

---

12 Consider 2 John 1:7–11: "For many deceivers have gone out into the world, those who do not confess the coming of Jesus Christ in the flesh. Such a one is the deceiver and the antichrist. Watch yourselves, so that you may not lose what we have worked for, but may win a full reward. Everyone who goes on ahead and does not abide in the teaching of Christ, does not have God. Whoever abides in the teaching has both the Father and the Son. If anyone comes to you and does not bring this teaching, do not receive him into your house or give him any greeting, for whoever greets him takes part in his wicked works." Although this passage warns against receiving a false teacher into your home, which would have implied a close, hospitable relationship of trust, it also suggests avoiding what might look like a potentially misleading relationship even out in the community.

to see. This might mean going quiet, moving out of sight, removing visible signs of ministry or worship, or perhaps all of the above. An example would be the so-called underground church in China, where millions of Christians worship in small cell groups, house churches, churches that are visible and tolerated by the communist authorities, or churches that register for the approval of the authorities and are granted an official status by the Communist government. Of course, as we work our way along this spectrum, the church is less and less out of sight, out of mind (i.e., less underground). Yet our Lord uses the whole spectrum of visibility to accomplish His plans. Another example would be the rumored but nearly impossible to substantiate claims of thousands of Muslims embracing faith in Christ in countries where such conversions carry a death sentence. The ministries that bring the Gospel to such areas typically avoid engaging their opponents because in many of these places their work of evangelism is a capital offense. Again, though, our Lord uses these ministries to reach many with the Gospel.

If other Christians have been forced to disengage and yet still continue their work, one way we can support them is to avoid highlighting or even mentioning them with any specifics that would draw the attention of potential persecutors. This can be tricky in the context of prayer and mutual support disciplines discussed in the previous chapter, but it is vital for the life of such covert ministries. Examples include taking care to avoid mentioning or providing names, photos, locations, or affiliations of missionaries in Nigeria, India, North Korea, or other countries where Christians could be targets for persecution by Muslims, Hindus, or communists.

Even if we need to disengage from a hostile situation, we still need to seek opportunities to continue Christian fellowship, mutual support, worship, and witness while avoiding as much hostility or persecution as possible. As we continue to plant the seed of the Gospel, even if done covertly or in more open parts of the community, God may use us to position the Church for dramatic growth if persecution diminishes at some future date. On the other hand, if we step back and drift into isolation rather than staying active, we risk becoming ingrown or even drifting off into false doctrine while isolated from other parts of the Church. As we consider this option and its pros and cons, we must also keep in mind God's desire to use us and our situation and seek His will for our course of action.

Play Better Defense

Sometimes, we run into hostility that is more intense than expected, or maybe something takes the situation past hostility and toward oppression, or perhaps the circumstances simply change in surprising ways. In other words, the situation is dynamic and maybe a bit more so than we expected. A fourth option, then, is to intentionally live according to Jesus' admonition in Matthew 10:16, where He said, "Behold, I am sending you out as sheep in the midst of wolves, so be wise as serpents and innocent as doves." His phrase "wise as serpents" suggests that we should be astute, shrewd, and prepared as we move forward with the Gospel and in ministry; "innocent as doves" suggests that our motives must be pure, reflecting God's sacrificial love rather than self-interest, even when we have reason to think the worst of our opposition. Jesus sends us out for ministry into areas where wolves may lurk and does not give us the choice of avoiding His work, so we need to be ready for hostile situations!

Playing better defense means keeping our head up and eyes open, being aware of what happens around us, so we can make the best of the situation, or make better use of the situation, as it evolves. This might be called tough-minded, but not callous-hearted. It requires what defense forces might call situational awareness. It involves sensitivity to words and events and requires shrewd critical thinking and creativity to be able to act proactively with God's interests in mind rather than just reacting with our own interests in mind. Christians who play a good defense are often one step ahead of their opposition, and they may look like they are at the top of their game. Of course, it is not really their game; it is God's game. This means taking a long view, a big-picture view, and making strategic moves, as in chess, thinking ahead about the implications and how things are likely to play out. Above all, and as noted before, we need to know the heart and mind of God.

Examples from the Bible include how Jesus adapted His plans seemingly on the fly as He anticipated and then recognized changing situations and growing opposition. In John 7:6–10, Jesus said to His not-too-friendly brothers, "'My time has not yet come, but your time is always here. The world cannot hate you, but it hates Me because I testify about it that its works are evil. You go up to the feast. I am not going up to this feast, for My time has not yet fully come.' After saying this, He remained in Galilee. But after His brothers had gone up to the feast, then He also went up, not publicly but in private." This first example might look like deception, but Jesus was taking steps to avoid disrupting His ministry before it was time for His cross, and any trip up to Jerusalem had to be done in a way that would avoid His premature arrest. Matthew 14:15–19 shows Jesus adapting His plans to meet the needs of the changing situation:

> Now when it was evening, the disciples came to Him and said, "This is a desolate place, and the day is now over; send the crowds away to go into the villages and buy food for themselves." But Jesus said, "They need not go away; you give them something to eat." They said to Him, "We have only five loaves here and two fish." And He said, "Bring them here to Me." Then He ordered the crowds to sit down on the grass, and taking the five loaves and the two fish, He looked up to heaven and said a blessing. Then He broke the loaves and gave them to the disciples, and the disciples gave them to the crowds.

In this case, Jesus was balancing the need to challenge and teach His disciples with His intent to not send the crowds away hungry. John 6:5–6 says, "Lifting up His eyes, then, and seeing that a large crowd was coming toward Him, Jesus said to Philip, 'Where are we to buy bread, so that these people may eat?' He said this to test him, for He Himself knew what He would do." Yes, Jesus knew what He would do, but He was still intentionally adapting His plans as the situation evolved.

David's behavior and deference to God's will while under Saul's persecution provide us with another good example: he was proactive rather than reactive, he was not opportunistic or prone to taking cheap shots, and he loved God in his heart and showed this with his actions. First Samuel 24:4–7 relates what happened when Saul unknowingly entered the cave where David and his men were hiding:

> And the men of David said to him, "Here is the day of which the Lord said to you, 'Behold, I will give your enemy into your hand, and you shall do to him as it shall seem good to you.'" Then David arose and stealthily cut off a corner of Saul's robe. And afterward David's heart struck him, because he had cut off a corner of Saul's robe. He said to his men, "The Lord forbid

that I should do this thing to my lord, the LORD's anointed, to put out my hand against him, seeing he is the LORD's anointed." So David persuaded his men with these words and did not permit them to attack Saul.

David had opportunity to take revenge on Saul, his persecutor, but instead of seizing that opportunity, he set an example for his men by leaving revenge to God rather than seeking his own legitimate interests.

Paul's behavior and attitude provide another good example: regardless of opposition, disaster, punishment, or any other impediment, he was always working to reach people with the Gospel. Think of Paul adapting his delivery without compromising the content of the Gospel when he was mocked and even accused of babbling in Athens. Acts 17:18 records, "Some of the Epicurean and Stoic philosophers also conversed with him. And some said, 'What does this babbler wish to say?' Others said, 'He seems to be a preacher of foreign divinities'—because he was preaching Jesus and the resurrection." Paul responded by adapting his stump speech to refer back to the God of creation, rather than starting with Old Testament prophecy as he usually did when speaking to the Jews, to set the stage for presenting the Gospel of Christ. As Paul wrapped up his presentation, Acts 17:32 relates, "Now when they heard of the resurrection of the dead, some mocked. But others said, 'We will hear you again about this.'" Paul's adapted approach succeeded in sowing the seed of God's Word, and God blessed his faithful confession as some members of the crowd came to faith and others wanted to hear more. In this dynamic situation as well as throughout his ministry, Paul's attitude was one of thanksgiving and praise, as innocent as a dove, even while remaining shrewd and strategic in his thinking.

Examples from today include Christians in Egypt finding ways to work with the Muslim government while steering clear of as much trouble as possible, avoiding alienating or offending their Muslim neighbors, and sometimes even winning sympathy and support from Islamic political leaders (e.g., Egyptian President Sisi speaking out in support of Christians in Egypt).[13] This strategy may work well in concert with some of the other

---

13 Jayson Casper, "Libya's 21 Christian Martyrs: 'With Their Blood, They Are Unifying Egypt,'" *Christianity Today*, February 18, 2015; Jayson Casper, "How Libya's Martyrs Are Witnessing to Egypt," *Christianity Today*, February 23, 2015; and Jamie Dean, "The ISIS war against 'the people of the cross.'" *WORLD News Group*, February 17, 2015.

options we consider in this chapter. Another example of heads-up, effective defense might be when Christians see and seize an opportunity to do the unexpected, such as extending kindness to a hostile person, complete strangers, or perhaps a secular news reporter. This happened a few years ago when a number of Chick-fil-A employees were found handing out food to motorists stuck in a snowstorm, and this after the company (which was owned and managed by Christians) had been roundly criticized in the secular news for supporting traditional marriage rather than homosexual marriage.[14] Such an unexpected display of kindness can startle onlookers and lead to opportunities for sharing God's grace and forgiveness.

Benefits of this shrewd/innocent approach include preserving and perhaps even extending Christian fellowship, ministry, and witness under difficult conditions; recognizing and avoiding trouble as much as can be done; and continuing a visible Christian presence in the community, even if parts of that community must be avoided. Another less tangible advantage involves maintaining the good will of most of our neighbors and allowing the dark nature of the opposition to make itself known through its hostility and intolerance. This potentially stark contrast actually helps validate the Gospel, make it more attractive, and even helps spread the Word. If carried too far or used thoughtlessly, though, playing such a heads-up defense can make Christians seem too calculating or manipulative. Non-believers sometimes think of Christians as naïve, meek, and sometimes uniformed, so when a well-informed, assertive, loving Christian engages the community, it is easy for the non-believers to miss or mistake the part of his behavior that includes "loving." To avoid inadvertently damaging our ministry and presence in the community, we need to balance shrewdness with innocence, both founded in the genuine love of our Savior.

Step Up the Proclamation

A proactive fifth alternative could include stepping up the proclamation of God's Word through preaching and teaching, complemented by works of service and acts of mercy, which can help defuse opposition. Stepping up

---

14   Andrew Branch, "Snow, shelter, and 'renewed' gospel perspective," *WORLD News Group*, January 31, 2014.

the proclamation of the Gospel involves mounting a stronger offense and might actually match the tough-minded, proactive defense discussed in the previous section. This approach benefits from imagination and creativity to identify new and emerging opportunities, an ability to articulate the love of Christ as the motive for what we are doing, an ability to share the Gospel in unusual settings and in one-on-one conversations, and a simple working understanding of apologetics. In summary, this strategy of increased, higher-profile activity focuses on countering the opposition with public arguments of apologetics and with deeds of service that may speak more loudly than words alone.

In effect, rather than leaving the playing field, we would redouble our efforts to take the Gospel of Christ into the community around us. Perhaps it is better to think of our surroundings as a harvest field, as Jesus suggests in John 4:35b: "Look, I tell you, lift up your eyes, and see that the fields are white for harvest." This approach can make Christianity more visible and more credible as a legitimate worldview in the eyes of the unchurched, who may know nothing of the Gospel except what they have heard from those who oppose Christ. In keeping with the Holy Spirit's delegation of gifts and responsibilities in the congregation, pastors, ministry staff, lay leadership, and members of the congregation all have roles to play in such a stepped-up effort. And it is important for the whole Body of Christ to be visibly involved rather than leaving one person, whether pastor or layman, alone on the playing field as a target for the enemy.

Acts 18:24–28 tells us,

> Now a Jew named Apollos, a native of Alexandria, came to Ephesus. He was an eloquent man, competent in the Scriptures. He had been instructed in the way of the Lord. And being fervent in spirit, he spoke and taught accurately the things concerning Jesus, though he knew only the baptism of John. He began to speak boldly in the synagogue, but when Priscilla and Aquila heard him, they took him aside and explained to him the way of God more accurately. And when he wished to cross to Achaia, the brothers encouraged him and wrote to the disciples to welcome him. When he arrived, he greatly helped those who through grace had believed, for he powerfully

refuted the Jews in public, showing by the Scriptures that the Christ was Jesus.

Countering opposition with arguments of apologetics involves making a reasoned defense through preaching and teaching based on Scripture, following the example of Apollos. We can draw two additional, useful insights from this account of Apollos, though. The first is that the local fellowship, through instruction by Priscilla and Aquila, was instrumental in bringing Apollos to full knowledge of the faith and in focusing his understanding to benefit the Church. The second insight is that once oriented and refocused, Apollos was instrumental in turning the situation around for the Christians in Achaia.[15] Of course, this points to the potential value of our efforts in this area.

We do not have to master every part of this as individuals, but we do need to know whom in the church or in our fellowship we can turn to for help if we run into a question or situation that we can't handle. And if we don't know an answer, we should simply say so and ask for time to come back with an answer later. When this happens, it is not a setback; it is an opportunity to earn credibility for our honesty and to step up our game.

The idea of complementing the arguments of apologetics with deeds of service derives from Jesus' command to love our neighbors coupled with His statement that our love for one another will validate our identity as Christ's disciples. In Mark 12:29–31, responding to a question about which is the most important commandment, Jesus answered, "The most important is, 'Hear, O Israel: The Lord our God, the Lord is one. And you shall love the Lord your God with all your heart and with all your soul and with all your mind and with all your strength.' The second is this: 'You shall love your neighbor as yourself.' There is no other commandment greater than these." Then in John 13:34–35, we see Jesus telling His disciples, "A new commandment I give to you, that you love one another: just as I have loved you, you also are to love one another. By this all people will know that you are My disciples, if you have love for one another." It is not too much of a stretch,

---

15 Acts 18:27b–28 says that Apollos "greatly helped those who through grace had believed, for he powerfully refuted the Jews in public, showing by the Scriptures that the Christ was Jesus." These were the same Jews who earlier, in Acts 18:12b–13, "made a united attack on Paul and brought him before the tribunal, saying, 'This man is persuading people to worship God contrary to the law.'"

then, to conclude that our manifestation of God's love will inevitably have an effect on our witness, on our fellowship, and on neighbors we serve. In fact, our Lord stakes our identity as His disciples on it!

Stepping up the proclamation, then, could involve seeking new venues for preaching and teaching, or it could involve looking for needs and service opportunities to improve the visibility of Christians and the church in the local community. New venues might include, for example, participating in ethical or policy reviews in local government or perhaps teaching classes on comparative religion, history of western civilization, apologetics, the Reformation, or church history at the local junior college, high school, or university. Service opportunities might include offering the church facilities as a venue for local theater or other performing arts organizations; joining local government advisory committees; supporting charity and support activities such as food banks, soup kitchens, or homeless shelters; participating in community cleanup days; teaching English as a second language; or tutoring students in local schools. The goal is to get out into the community where Jesus is already working to prepare hearts for the Gospel.

Advantages of stepping up the proclamation include reaching more people with God's love and the Gospel; increasing Christian presence, visibility, and credibility in the local community; strengthening Christian fellowship and teamwork as we work together; and improving our readiness (e.g., critical thinking ability) for questions and challenges. In some cases, we may win unexpected allies in the process. In addition to visibility, name recognition, and credibility for our Christian group, these interactions also provide a grassroots venue to influence community values and opinions. The main downsides, particularly if we don't follow through once started, include becoming a more obvious target for opposition, the cost in terms of time and energy, and the risk of drifting off into a social gospel if we fail to hold to God's truth as the core of our confession.

Make Common Cause

Another possible option involves finding common ground or making common cause with other groups, whether secular or religious. Paul used this strategy before the ruling council in Jerusalem, playing the Pharisees off against the Sadducees, with the Pharisees taking Paul's side. Acts 23:6–10 explains,

> Now when Paul perceived that one part were Sadducees and the other Pharisees, he cried out in the council, "Brothers, I am a Pharisee, a son of Pharisees. It is with respect to the hope and the resurrection of the dead that I am on trial." And when he had said this, a dissension arose between the Pharisees and the Sadducees, and the assembly was divided. For the Sadducees say that there is no resurrection, nor angel, nor spirit, but the Pharisees acknowledge them all. Then a great clamor arose, and some of the scribes of the Pharisees' party stood up and contended sharply, "We find nothing wrong in this man. What if a spirit or an angel spoke to him?" And when the dissension became violent, the tribune, afraid that Paul would be torn to pieces by them, commanded the soldiers to go down and take him away from among them by force and bring him into the barracks.

In addition to Paul's maneuver in playing the Pharisees off against the Sadducees, Paul found an unexpected ally in Gallio (Acts 18:12–17), who refused to let the Jews in Corinth bring Paul to trial over matters of the faith. Acts 18:12–16 relates what happened:

> When Gallio was proconsul of Achaia, the Jews made a united attack on Paul and brought him before the tribunal, saying, "This man is persuading people to worship God contrary to the law." But when Paul was about to open his mouth, Gallio said to the Jews, "If it were a matter of wrongdoing or vicious crime, O Jews, I would have reason to accept your complaint. But since it is a matter of questions about words and names and your own law, see to it yourselves. I refuse to be a judge of these things." And he drove them from the tribunal.

169

So in one case, Paul found an ally in one religious group (Pharisees) that would take his side against another group. In the second case, one of the ruling authorities intervened in an unexpected way that blocked accusations against Paul. For our situations, though, we should probably take a broadly based approach, since we do not know very far in advance who might take which side in a situation involving religious freedom, oppression, or persecution. We may seek allies based on what we know of the position taken by other religious groups or individuals, they may seek us, or we may find each other through independent third-party groups such as Alliance Defending Freedom.[16] Teaming up provides more leverage as we attempt to push back against hostility and oppression and as we attempt to influence our situation and its outcome.

As we apply our rights as citizen through the courts, election campaigns, or other efforts to influence public opinion, policy, or the law, we may find that other groups share our view on the issue at hand and are willing to team with us for the same goal. These other groups may be Christian, secular, or even from other religions. For example, the Mormon Church (Latter Day Saints [LDS]) recently filed a friend of the court brief with the U.S. Supreme Court in an attempt to influence their decision on the legalities of gay marriage. Because The Lutheran Church—Missouri Synod (LCMS) and LDS have common interests in defending marriage between one man and one woman—the way God originally designed marriage as being the only norm for legitimate marriage—they have become partners in this effort, an event that would otherwise be unlikely.[17]

A common-ground strategy, therefore, might usefully involve working with other groups to invoke our rights of citizenship and mobilize public opinion against those who would impede or attack Christian witness and service. Recent examples of this strategy include joint statements by The Lutheran Church—Missouri Synod with Catholic, Jewish, and Muslim organizations, all concerned about issues affecting freedom of religion.[18]

---

16 See Appendix 1 for more information about Alliance Defending Freedom.

17 Ben Winslow, "LDS Church asks U.S. Supreme Court to rule against same-sex marriage," *Fox News*, April 10, 2015.

18 See Matthew Harrison, "Free Exercise of Religion: Putting Beliefs into Practice, An Open Letter from Religious Leaders in the United States to All Americans," June 21, 2012.

Liberal social policies (e.g., abortion, sexuality, or gender-related issues) at major medical associations have become difficult for many conservative and Christian doctors to accept, so some are fighting back by organizing alternative professional groups.[19] However, for Christian organizations and churches, this kind of approach needs careful development and implementation to avoid creating collateral problems or compromising God's truth. We must keep the Gospel as our priority, rather than political success.[20]

Making common cause with other individuals and groups can enhance our influence on public opinion and political processes. Another advantage would be the opportunity to check what we believe and to offer a confession of faith to our newfound allies. On the other hand, collaborating with other groups carries the risk of confusing observers about what we know and believe in comparison with what our allies believe. And as we share our credibility with the other group, there is the risk of inadvertently giving them a degree of legitimacy that they do not deserve. We can manage these concerns by maintaining clear communications and expectations and by not letting the scope of our collaboration grow out of control.

Take Our Leave

If all else fails as we face opposition or persecution, there may come a time when we need to shake the dust off our feet, leave the community, and take the Gospel to another location. This is somewhat related to the third option above, which involved disengaging from a difficult situation, but this specifically means relocating to a new community to continue sharing the Gospel and it may mean God's judgment on the place we leave behind. This is a serious matter. God's judgment in these situations probably means God letting them go, leaving them to their own devices. We see this judgment in Romans 1:24, 26, and 28, for example, where each verse includes the chilling phrase, "God gave them up . . ."

Jesus explained the alternative of taking our leave when He sent the twelve disciples out as sheep among wolves and instructed them on how to respond according to whether their ministry was received or rejected. In

---

19 Daniel James Devine, "Second opinions," *WORLD News Group*, June 14, 2014.

20 The Commission on Theology and Church Relations, *Principles for Cooperation in Externals with Theological Integrity* (St. Louis: The Lutheran Church—Missouri Synod, 2011).

Matthew 10:5–7, 11–15, we read,

> These twelve Jesus sent out, instructing them, "Go nowhere among the Gentiles and enter no town of the Samaritans, but go rather to the lost sheep of the house of Israel. And proclaim as you go, saying, 'The kingdom of heaven is at hand.' . . . And whatever town or village you enter, find out who is worthy in it and stay there until you depart. As you enter the house, greet it. And if the house is worthy, let your peace come upon it, but if it is not worthy, let your peace return to you. And if anyone will not receive you or listen to your words, shake off the dust from your feet when you leave that house or town. Truly, I say to you, it will be more bearable on the day of judgment for the land of Sodom and Gomorrah than for that town."

It is important to realize that although the disciples could disengage, shake the dust off of their feet, and leave if they and God's Word were rejected, Jesus expected them to move on and take up ministry in a new location rather than simply quit. In Matthew 10:23, Jesus said, "When they persecute you in one town, flee to the next, for truly, I say to you, you will not have gone through all the towns of Israel before the Son of Man comes." The notion of going through all the towns did not mean playing tourist; it meant taking God's Word to each town, one after the other. And the idea that they would not finish before the return of Christ (the Son of Man) tells us that there are plenty of towns (mission fields) left to work. So, in that vein, if we disengage and leave a community, we should expect God to put us to work in Christian ministry in the community we come to next. The fields are ripe for harvest, and we should always expect to be at work in one mission field or another. Acts 8:1, 4 show this in action at the time of the first great persecution and exile from Jerusalem: "And there arose on that day a great persecution against the church in Jerusalem, and they were all scattered throughout the regions of Judea and Samaria, except the apostles. . . . Now those who were scattered went about preaching the word." God scattered the Christians from Jerusalem so that they could preach (scatter) the Gospel wherever they were. This was the next step in fulfilling our Lord's command in the Great Commission: "He said to them, 'It is not for you to know times or seasons that the Father has fixed by His own authority. But you will receive power when the Holy Spirit has come upon you, and you will be My witnesses in Jerusalem and in all Judea and Samaria, and to the end of the earth'" (Acts 1:7–8). It is both fascinating and humbling to think how God scatters us like seeds, expecting us to sow His Word by sharing the Gospel.

Examples in the New Testament include the disciples in Matthew 10, who no doubt took Jesus' words to heart. A second example of leaving the scene comes up in Acts 9:23–25, which relates, "When many days had passed, the Jews plotted to kill him, but their plot became known to Saul. They were watching the gates day and night in order to kill him, but his disciples took him by night and let him down through an opening in the wall, lowering him in a basket." Saul (Paul) had help from friends, whom he seems to have left behind to continue ministry while staying below the attention of the persecutors (our "Disengage" option on pp. 158–61). A third example appears in Acts 13:49–51, which says, "And the word of the Lord was spreading throughout the whole region. But the Jews incited the devout women of high standing and the leading men of the city, stirred up persecution against Paul and Barnabas, and drove them out of their district. But they shook off the dust from their feet against them and went to Iconium." In this case, Paul and Barnabas apparently shook off the dust from their feet against the part of the community that persecuted them but not against other parts of the community that were receptive to the Gospel.

Present-day examples include Christians who fled from Muslim terrorists (ISIS) in Syria, Iraq, or Nigeria[1] and Christians who escape from North Korea.[2] In each case, this has meant the loss of Christian witness and presence from community after community, and for the most part, these examples have involved Christians fleeing for their lives and becoming

---

1   Ron Prosor, "The Middle East War on Christians," *The Wall Street Journal*, April 16, 2014; Leslie Loftis, "Don't Close Your Eyes To Christians Purged and Tortured in Iraq," *The Federalist*, August 1, 2014; Mindy Belz, "Forgotten survivors," *WORLD News Group*, November 26, 2014; and Sam Dagher, "Middle East Christians Trapped by Islamist Extremists Forge Alliances With Former Foes," *The Wall Street Journal*, April 13, 2015, all provide recent examples of Christians who had to leave their homes because of persecution. The news sources listed in Appendix 1 can provide examples that are more current.

2   Julia A. Seymour, "U.S. government: Worldwide religious intolerance growing," *WORLD News Group*, May 6, 2014; and "Tier 1 Countries of Particular Concern," United States Commission on International Religious Freedom (www.uscirf.gov/all-countries/countries-of-particular-concern-tier-1).

refugees rather than simply leaving for ministry in the next town. Yet their presence in a new community, or even in a refugee camp, means moving some degree of Christian influence into a new location. In a much less dire situation, anecdotal evidence suggests that some Christians are choosing to move away from parts of the United States that are not very family-friendly in order to have a better opportunity to raise their children in the faith. Again, this marks a loss for the areas left behind, but it works to the advantage of the Christian's new home communities.

So what might taking our leave look like for us? Taking our leave from where we are oppressed or persecuted involves physically leaving the opposition, possibly temporarily but more likely in a permanent move. We might be able to sell out, pack up, and completely move away; we might simply pack a bag and leave; or we might have to run away on very short notice with only the clothes on our backs. Ordinarily, it is a given that we would take our family with us, but if we see the situation as coming and inevitable, we might send them away ahead of our escape. Of course, all of this depends on timing and circumstances that are largely out of our control but that are certainly within God's reach.

Advantages of leaving include preserving our safety and taking the Gospel, our Christian presence, and resources to another location. The downside, of course, is that we are removing our Christian confession from a location that sorely needs it. Other implications include the risk of placing a potentially inordinate amount of emphasis on the decision to leave or stay, rather than allowing us to focus completely on sharing the Gospel. We must seek God's council and guidance on our choices so that we can minimize negative impacts on our opportunities to share the Gospel.

Stay and Endure

Coming full circle from our original discussion of turning the other cheek, we may elect to stay where we are, stick it out, and endure the suffering. The difference might be that turning the other cheek implies a temporary or one-of-a-kind situation while staying and enduring implies persevering for an indefinite time through an ongoing hostility or persecution. In its simplest form, for us to stay and endure means sticking it out to the end, even if the level of uncertainty adds to the difficulties. Regardless, we would continue our spiritual disciplines and, as opportunities permit, our confession of faith to our persecutors and neighbors.

The world around us will often view our sticking it out as a frustrating and probably wasted effort—a poor choice by any "reasonable" criteria, and certainly not one in keeping with conventional worldly wisdom about a life well lived. Hebrews 11:38, wrapping up a review of heroes of the faith, points to these differences in values and understanding when it describes the faithful as those "of whom the world was not worthy." Our neighbors would probably see our plight as costing time and talent that could have been invested more profitably elsewhere, if they see the situation at all. After all, our suffering may or may not be visible to others as we stay and endure. It may come to light later, just as the magnitude of the Holocaust in World War II was not fully understood until later, or it may conceivably never come to light. Yet God often uses hostile situations to demonstrate His power in ways that we might not expect. For example, in the Old Testament, God's punishment of Egypt taught other nations about His majesty, power, and justice, even though God's people (Israel) may not have understood this very well at the time.[3]

To stay and endure does not mean defeat or reflect a passive submission. In 1 Corinthians 16:8–9, Paul writes, "But I will stay in Ephesus until Pentecost, for a wide door for effective work has opened to me, and there are many adversaries." Think about what he is

> To stay and endure does not mean defeat or reflect a passive submission.

---

3   In 1 Samuel 6:6, the Philistine priests and diviners admonish the people, "Why should you harden your hearts as the Egyptians and Pharaoh hardened their hearts? After he had dealt severely with them, did they not send the people away, and they departed?" Apparently, word had spread regarding how God delivered Israel from Egyptian persecution.

saying here: he will stick around to preach and teach because there is an open door for ministry, plus opposition. It almost sounds like the opposition is an unexpected bonus! There are two reasons why Paul might think this way: First, any place the Holy Spirit is working, the evil one will raise up opposition. It is a safe bet that Paul preferred to be in ministry where the Holy Spirit is working. Second, Paul also felt a sense of responsibility for those he reached with the Gospel, and particularly for the churches he planted. We see this in Acts 15:36, for example, where "Paul said to Barnabas, 'Let us return and visit the brothers in every city where we proclaimed the word of the Lord, and see how they are.'" If Paul, in Ephesus, knew that the church faced adversaries, he would want to stay to help the church face the opposition. Regardless of which reason was predominant, Paul wanted to stay and work. In Matthew 5:16, Jesus said, "Let your light shine before others, so that they may see your good works and give glory to your Father who is in heaven." God gains glory when we demonstrate that we care more for Him, His work, and His people than we do for avoiding persecution. We could do a lot worse than to follow Paul's example.

Additional examples from the New Testament would include Christians who stayed behind in various cities after persecution arose. Acts 13:51–52 says, "They [Paul and Barnabas] shook off the dust from their feet against them and went to Iconium. And the disciples were filled with joy and with the Holy Spirit," indicating that a body of believers was left behind in Antioch. Acts 14:19–20a relates, "But Jews came from Antioch and Iconium, and having persuaded the crowds, they stoned Paul and dragged him out of the city, supposing that he was dead. But when the disciples gathered about him, he rose up and entered the city," indicating again that a body of believers had been planted, this time in Lystra. And Acts 16:40 says, "So they went out of the prison and visited Lydia. And when they had seen the brothers, they encouraged them and departed." This narrative shows that Paul left behind a startup church in Philippi after being jailed for his ministry. We do not know what happened next with each of these churches, but simply note that Christians stayed and endured after opposition arose and after Paul left for other mission opportunities.

Present day examples include those Christians who stay behind in areas of Iraq,[4] Syria,[5] Nigeria,[6] Pakistan,[7] India,[8] Ukraine,[9] and other countries[10] even as Muslim forces, Hindu extremists, or communists and their allies pressure their communities with hostility or persecution. In areas where persecutors have taken over, the remaining Christians keep a low profile, out of necessity, but still have influence in the community and in supporting one another. Their endurance in their homes or in refugee camps under the most extreme kinds of suffering is remarkable evidence of faith and a sign of God preserving a remnant of His faithful. Adjacent areas threatened by persecution may not be that much easier as a place to live, but the Christians there have an opportunity to continue a visible presence, prepare for the worst, and pray for the future. In some cases, preparing for the worst has included acquiring weapons to defend families and communities against invading persecutors,[11] but self-defense is not always possible.

Staying and enduring can provide a strong witness to neighboring families or even worldwide, depending on whether the full account ever gets out to others. Enduring can also be a character-building experience that God uses to refine and strengthen us, much as a metallurgist heats and forges steel to make it tough and strong. However, even though we often hear that

---

4   Tamara Audi, "Iraqi Christians' Dilemma: Stay or Go?" *The Wall Street Journal*, September 29, 2014.

5   Raja Abdulrahim, "Islamic State Militants Seize Christians, Villages in Northeast Syria," *The Wall Street Journal*, February 24, 2015.

6   Julia A. Seymour, "Boko Haram expanding from Nigeria to Cameroon," *WORLD News Group*, September 22, 2014; Drew Hinshaw, "Boko Haram Rampages, Slaughters in Northeast Nigeria," *The Wall Street Journal*, January 9, 2015; and Patrick McGroarty and Heidi Vogt, "Violence Between Christian, Muslims Poses New Challenge in Nigeria," *The Wall Street Journal*, April 12, 2015.

7   Julia A. Seymour, "Pakistan reinstates death penalty, Christians fear blasphemy charges," *WORLD News Group*, March 16, 2015.

8   Julia A. Seymour, "India's Christians protest after St. Sebastian's Church burns," *WORLD News Group*, December 8, 2014; and Suryatapa Bhattacharya, "Christians Say Break-In a Sign of Rising Religious Intolerance in Delhi," *The Wall Street Journal*, February 3, 2015.

9   Julia A. Seymour, "Persecution grows in rebel-held regions of Ukraine," *WORLD News Group*, March 23, 2015.

10 Ned Levin, "Hong Kong Democracy Protests Carry a Christian Mission for Some," *The Wall Street Journal*, October 3, 2014.

11 Rachel Lynn Aldrich, "Lebanese Christians take up arms as ISIS terror spreads," *WORLD News Group*, September 5, 2014; Nour Malas, "Iraq's Christians Take Up Arms to Fight Islamic State," *The Wall Street Journal*, February 3, 2015; and Sam Dagher, "Middle East Christians Trapped by Islamist Extremists Forge Alliances With Former Foes," *The Wall Street Journal*, April 13, 2015.

persecution strengthens and grows the church, it is important to be realistic and recall that sometimes a local or even a regional church might not survive. Revelation 2 and 3 speak to seven of the early churches, but how many of these are thriving centers of Christianity today? It may be true that a visible part of the church, one that we can see with our own eyes, is in serious trouble and under persecution. If persecution becomes so severe that it wipes out even an enduring visible minority of Christians, we must give God the glory, remember that He is in charge, and pray for the day to come when He would reseed the persecuted area with His Word. Or we can pray for the imminent return of our Lord Jesus Christ, but perhaps it would be best if we pray both for His reseeding and for His return and leave the details up to Him.

God cuts a wide swath (wider than we can see) and takes a long view (longer than we can endure), and His plans must prevail. We can rest in the assurance that, as Isaiah 55:10–11 promises, "as the rain and the snow come down from heaven and do not return there but water the earth, making it bring forth and sprout, giving seed to the sower and bread to the eater, so shall My word be that goes out from My mouth; it shall not return to Me empty, but it shall accomplish that which I purpose, and shall succeed in the thing for which I sent it."

⌘⌘

Discussion Questions

1. In this chapter we discussed several different options for responding to hostility and persecution. Have you ever responded to hostility with one of these tactics? If so, which one did you use and why?

2. Do you feel like your rights as a Christian citizen are eroding? How so, and what will you do about it?

3. Have you ever encountered unexpected allies when facing hostility for your faith? Who were they, and how did you help one another?

4. What does it mean to you to be as shrewd as a serpent and as innocent as a dove?

5. Have you experienced a situation where you had to choose between obeying governing authorities and obeying God? Explain.

6

Gospel-Based Guidance

The spiritual disciplines we discussed in chapter 4 give us a broad, strong foundation for facing hostility, oppression, or persecution, regardless of the details of our situation. But looking beyond those basics, how do we choose from among the options outlined in chapter 5?

Each situation differs in its circumstances and in its dynamic, in the personalities that are involved and in their motives. We may be directly in the middle of it, or we may be watching from a distance, or we may see a threat emerging and coming in our direction. Each situation also has its own timeline. Hostility might be temporary and perhaps a one-time event, or it may arise repeatedly at irregular intervals, or it may be ongoing for an indefinite length of time. The challenge might arise quickly, even overnight, or it might take shape slowly and potentially with plenty of advance warning. These aspects of a situation all affect our range of choices and how quickly we need to take action (or if we decide to take action at all), but they should not have as much influence as Christ-centered underlying motives and priorities that shape our thinking.

God is our rock, according to the psalmist, so we are not on shaky ground. Thus, to move from abstract to application, what motives and priorities should guide how we see the situation and how we decide our course of action? When we face hostility, oppression, or persecution, we need to respond proactively rather than reacting out of fear or self-interest. This is almost always a situational thing, in that the circumstances of each situation will be a little different (or maybe a lot different) and we need to deal with what is happening rather than reliving past experience. So how do we decide what to do, given the options we have been discussing? To be able to respond in a proactive, God-pleasing way, we need to realize that God has already given us some power over the situation and some sense of His priorities for guidance. This is our basis for discerning the path forward.

First, know that God has given us power of forgiveness. He entrusts His people with the Office of the Keys and, as spelled out in the Lord's Prayer, expects to forgive us as we forgive others. What kind of power does forgiveness have over our persecutors? Try changing "power" to "authority" and ask the question again. It is the living God who ultimately has authority and power to forgive, and He delegates that authority and power to us. By forgiving our enemies, we are not claiming that we have power over them (even though in that sense we do have power), but we are definitely reminding them in a loving way that they are not really in charge. We gently remind them that our God is in control.

> **God has given us power of forgiveness.**

What we do with the power of forgiveness reflects how we understand and live according to God's Law and Gospel, so we need to take care that we do not put our own interests ahead of what God would like to do with our opponents as well as with our neighbors. Our neighbors need God's grace and forgiveness, as do our opponents. It is fine to pray for the defeat of our enemies, but we also need to pray for their repentance and salvation. But what does it do to our confession of the Gospel if we are reluctant to forgive? We are Christians, or "little Christs," so what we do reflects directly on how people perceive our Savior.

Second, know that we have the power of moral authority. We do not create this power on our own, but it comes from the fact that we are strongly identified with Christ as individuals and as the Church and because people can see Christ living in us. Our power of moral authority is less tangible than our power to forgive, but it is real nevertheless. Maybe this is like goodwill—hard to measure, but you know when you don't have it! Yet we as Christians do have moral authority. God has given us His Word, and we know the living God, the Creator and Lord of the universe, on a first-name basis. Since we bear this authority, our choices and behaviors will necessarily affect our credibility and confession of the Gospel. Actions often speak louder than words, so our choices and behavior will affect how people view or receive the name of Jesus and His Gospel. We need to choose wisely with God's wisdom and with an eye toward the implications of our choices.

Centrality of the Gospel

We need to know the heart and mind of God—ultimately, this is our basis for discerning how we as Christians respond to hostility and persecution. We learn the heart and mind of God in His Word, the Bible, and through His Son, Jesus Christ.[1] So from what we have studied of the heart and mind of God, what does God hope of us? Or if hope is the wrong word, what does He expect, or what would He like to see us do?

Scientists and philosophers sometimes use a tool known as Occam's razor to sort and choose among competing solutions to a problem. Simply put, Occam's razor calls for choosing the alternative that answers the question and fits the available information with the fewest assumptions and simplest explanation. Borrowing the concept, we can propose a Gospel razor to help us discern the path forward: When faced with hostility, opposition, or persecution, which response is the most authentic to Christ's ministry of the cross? Which course of action best suits the Gospel? Which choices bring glory to God?

This question has come up many times in the history of the Church, and it will continue to arise to challenge you, me, and other Christians all over the world. After experiencing arrests, jail time, trials, and beatings, Peter and other apostles persevered in teaching and preaching Jesus as the Christ.

---

1 Hebrews 1:1–3 points to the richness of this revelation by saying, "Long ago, at many times and in many ways, God spoke to our fathers by the prophets, but in these last days He has spoken to us by His Son, whom He appointed the heir of all things, through whom also He created the world. He is the radiance of the glory of God and the exact imprint of His nature, and He upholds the universe by the word of His power. After making purification for sins, He sat down at the right hand of the Majesty on high."

Stephen was arrested, tried, and executed, yet throughout his ordeal he confessed the Gospel of Christ and forgave those who took up stones against him. Paul endured almost every kind of hostility imaginable, but nothing could shake him from living and sharing Christ's Gospel. When hostility comes to us, what will we do?

Consider once again that God has placed us in the Body of Christ to perform certain roles according to His will and according to the gifts given us by the Holy Spirit. Consider that He has positioned each of us in the world as part of a diaspora, as He seeds the world with little Christs. Consider that He sent His Son, as

When hostility comes to us, what will we do?

described in John 3:16, knowing in advance that Jesus would become the blood sacrifice offered to redeem us, simply and profoundly because of His great love for us. Finally, consider that we are Christians ("little Christs") in God's plans. Taken together, what does all of this mean for how we respond to hostility, oppression, or persecution? How we answer that question really is all about Jesus and not about us. So what will you do?

⌘⌘

Discussion Questions

1. God sent His Son to die for us so that we could be saved. He calls us to imitate Christ, but what does this mean for you if you encounter persecution?

2. Have you ever found it hard to forgive someone? How did you get over it?

3. Do you know anyone who seems opposed to Christ out of a sense of guilt? What could you do to share God's grace with them?

4. What do you think God would like you to do if you face persecution? If you are too weak to do this on your own (you are), what choices do you have?

5. What priorities would shape your choices of how to respond to hostility? How would this reflect God's priorities and authority over the situation?

7

Concluding Thoughts

When we encounter hostility, opposition, or persecution, we need to identify scriptural and situation-appropriate strategies and courses of action for proactive responses. This means acting in an informed, spiritually discerning way rather than reacting out of self-interest. As we have seen, this really means that we act in accord with God's will and God's love, the mind and heart of God, rather than attempting to solve the problem on our own. Several common threads emerge when we consider the options in light of Scripture. As Peter exhorts in his first letter, we must stand fast and remain faithful, seeking God's direction and strength to respond properly to challenges as they come. The basic spiritual disciplines of prayer, self-examination, forgiveness, witness, mutual support, and knowing what we believe (better yet, knowing both what we believe and Him who we believe!) will help us discern and follow God's will for the path forward. Above all, our choices must imitate Christ as we take up our cross and follow Him.

The Amish story we considered earlier underscores the potential impact of our choices. To recap, in October 2006, a gunman entered an Amish schoolhouse in Pennsylvania, murdered five schoolgirls, and then committed suicide. During the chaos that followed, and in the midst of their suffering, Amish community leaders visited the gunman's widow and parents. They did not diminish the magnitude of the sin, nor did they offer cheap grace, but they offered forgiveness. Amazed by such an uncommon thing, the news media reported this story worldwide. We can only wonder at how many openings it created to discuss the reality of sin, the reality of God's grace, our need to forgive and to be forgiven, and the power of the Gospel of Jesus Christ.

More recently, in February 2015, members of ISIS, a self-declared Muslim caliphate, beheaded twenty-one Christians on the shores of the Mediterranean Sea because the Christians would not renounce their faith. ISIS videotaped the execution to make an example of it and released the video worldwide. In the audio, the Christians could be heard praying aloud to Jesus in the moments just before they were martyred. This provided the world with a demonstration of the reality of evil, the strength of the Christian faith, and the fact that some of us are willing to die for that faith. Again, we can only wonder at how God is already using an event like this to reach people with the Gospel of Jesus Christ.

We gather around His cross, receive His grace, and then take up our cross to follow Him. We live in the power of His Gospel, and God can use our response to hostility to reach those He would save. As Christians, we live in a God-driven diaspora, placed where He wants us. With this in mind, we thank God for the honor of being in His service, seize the opportunities He provides for witness, and stand firm in Christ!

⌘⌘

Appendices

Appendix 1
Sources of Additional Information

We usually find the most current information about religious freedom, hostility, oppression, and persecution on the Internet, thus all of the resources listed here are available online. The first set of resources includes several nongovernment organizations (NGOs) and then U.S. government organizations. Many of the NGOs reflect Christian values and perspectives, while those with the U.S. government are clearly and sometimes frustratingly secular in nature. Each listing includes a short comment to introduce the organization, a summary statement from that organization's website, and its Web address for further information.

As you skim through the materials, you will find that each organization has its own areas of interest, areas of coverage, strengths, perspectives, and limitations. Some are more outspoken than others, some tend to be more academic or more applied than others, some will ask you for money while others do not, and some are policy-centric while others are more hands-on. Each one seems to take a somewhat different view of the world around us, and you should approach this variety and these contrasts as a rich mix of resources rather than as competing interests. More information is better than none at all, so you may want to visit more than one resource, and revisit periodically, to really stay abreast of developments and their implications.

Nongovernment Organizations (in alphabetical order)

21st Century Wilberforce Initiative: A relatively new organization formed by a former U.S. congressman and a Christian pastor to advocate for religious freedom and for relief from persecution. Their vision is "to create a world where everyone embraces religious freedom as a universal right. The 21st Century Wilberforce Initiative champions religious freedom, the bedrock of human rights protection. Partnering with like-minded organizations and ministries, we seek awakening and transformation through education, technology, mobilization, and humanitarian assistance. There has never been a greater need both in history and scope. The rise of ISIS, the declining freedom of speech and communication globally, and the sheer number of religious prisoners around the world pose a critical threat to all of humanity. 21st Century Wilberforce wants to awaken the church to these atrocities and stir Christians and other religious groups to action." More information is available online at www.21wilberforce.org.

Alliance Defending Freedom: An organization of mostly Christian attorneys and support staff who use legal actions and information campaigns to support U.S. constitutional freedoms of speech, assembly, and religion. The organization has Christian roots and takes a liberal view of our freedoms, where "liberal" should be understood in a classical rather than political sense. Their website states that "Alliance Defending Freedom is an alliance-building legal organization that advocates for the right of people to freely live out their faith. Recognizing the need for a strong, coordinated legal defense against growing attacks on religious freedom, more than 30 prominent Christian leaders launched Alliance Defending Freedom in 1994. Over the past 20 years, this unique legal organization has brought together thousands of Christian attorneys and like-minded organizations that work tirelessly to advocate for the right of people to freely live out their faith in America and around the world." More information is available online at www.alliancedefendingfreedom.org.

The Becket Fund: A group of attorneys and support staff who use legal cases and the courts to support U.S. constitutional freedoms of religion and the associated constitutional freedoms of speech and assembly. According to their website, "the Becket Fund for Religious Liberty is a non-profit, public-interest legal and educational institute with a mission to protect the free expression of all faiths. The Becket Fund exists to vindicate a simple but frequently neglected principle: that because the religious impulse is natural to human beings, religious expression is natural to human culture. We advance that principle in three arenas— the courts of law, the court of public opinion, and the academy—both in the United States and abroad. At the Becket Fund we like to say we've defended the religious rights of people from 'A to Z,' from Anglicans to Zoroastrians. Our supporters represent a myriad of religions, but they all share our common vision of a world where religious freedom is respected as a fundamental human right that all are entitled to enjoy and exercise." More information is available online at www.becketfund.org.

Christian Freedom International: A nondenominational ministry to Christians facing hostility, oppression, and persecution. This is also a clearinghouse for information about what is happening in other countries and typically includes news that may not ever show up in traditional news media. Their website states, "The mission of Christian Freedom International is to help Christians who are persecuted and suffering for their faith in Jesus Christ. We are a non-denominational human rights organization providing real solutions to conditions of oppression and misery caused by religious persecution. We reach the part of the persecuted Church that is the most repressed, most at risk, and most isolated. In areas of disaster, we provide immediate relief to Christians, and their communities, who are ignored by conventional aid organizations. It is our privilege to minister to the Persecuted through Bible distribution, medical aid, resettlement assistance, advocacy, asylum case-work, and aid to the disabled; to sponsor schools, vocational training, and self-help initiatives; to provide these services at no charge by CFI staff and volunteers. It is our goal to work together with Christians at home to ease the burdens of our struggling brethren around the world." More information is available online at www.christianfreedom.org.

In Defense of Christians: A nondenominational ministry on behalf of Christians under oppression and persecution. This ministry tends to focus on policy issues rather than ministry directly to the persecuted, so it fills an important gap in that regard. Parts of their website are out of date at the time of this writing, but like the other nongovernmental organizations mentioned here, most of their money probably goes into their work rather than into their website. According to their website, "In Defense of Christians (IDC) is a non-profit, non-partisan organization whose mission is to heighten awareness among policymakers and the general public of the existence of ancient and often persecuted minority communities in the Middle East, particularly Christians. IDC will also conduct policy advocacy for vulnerable Christians and other religious minorities. Through greater awareness and advocacy, IDC hopes to influence the U.S. and foreign governments to adopt policies that will safeguard and empower minority religious communities in the Middle East, especially those vulnerable to violence, marginalization, and persecution." More information is available online at www.indefenseofchristians.org.

Lutheran Church—Missouri Synod: A confessional, evangelical Lutheran denomination with a strong network of congregations, schools, universities, seminaries, international and national missions, and support organizations. Their website states, "The LCMS launched an education and awareness campaign called 'Religious Liberty: Free to be Faithful' in September 2012 to protect American citizens' freedom of religion, to maintain the rights afforded in the Constitution for future generations, and to respond to increasing intrusions by government in the realm of the church. The campaign's main goal is to educate and move LCMS rostered members and laity to take informed action to protect religious freedom and all the cultural issues that pertain to it: the definition of marriage, the work of social service organizations, confessing the faith in the public square, aspects of the Health and Human Services mandate and the like." More information is available online at www.lcms.org/freetobefaithful.

Open Doors USA: A nondenominational ministry to Christians facing hostility, oppression, and persecution. This is also a clearinghouse for information about what is happening in other countries and typically includes news that may not ever show up in traditional news media. Their website includes a very good set of suggestions on how to help beyond just contributing money, praying, or signing petitions. It states, "For 60 years, Open Doors has worked in the world's most oppressive countries, empowering Christians who are persecuted for their beliefs. Open Doors equips persecuted Christians in more than 60 countries through programs like Bible & Gospel Development, Women & Children Advancement, and Christian Community Restoration." More information is available online at www.opendoorsusa.org.

Pew Research Center: The Pew Research Center is a reputable nongovernmental organization that develops and publishes a wide range of high-quality, independent research and social sciences information. Pew's Religion and Public Life project provides very good data and analysis of trends both within and affecting religions in the United States and around the world. It is important to realize that the analysis reflects big-picture developments that set a context for the more personal and more local accounts that other organizations provide. Pew's information often comes across as understated rather than sensationalized, but the quality is so good that their findings are often quoted in research studies, news articles, and policy analysis articles written by other organizations. More information is available online at www.pewforum.org.

Voice of the Martyrs: One of the oldest nondenominational Christian organizations dedicated to supporting the oppressed and persecuted. Their mission statement sums up their reason for existing: "Serving persecuted Christians through practical and spiritual assistance and leading other members of the Body of Christ into fellowship with them." Their website states, "The Voice of the Martyrs is a non-profit, inter-denominational Christian organization dedicated to assisting our persecuted family worldwide. VOM was founded in 1967 by Pastor Richard Wurmbrand, who was imprisoned 14 years in Communist Romania for his faith in Christ. His wife, Sabina, was imprisoned for three years. In the 1960s, Richard, Sabina, and their son, Mihai, were ransomed out of Romania and came to the United States. Through their travels, the Wurmbrands spread the message of the atrocities that Christians face in restricted nations, while establishing a network of offices dedicated to assisting the persecuted church." More information is available online at www.persecution.com.

U.S. Government Organizations (in alphabetical order)

U.S. Commission on International Religious Freedom (USCIRF): A government-funded organization whose levels of visibility and effectiveness may reflect presidential and congressional priorities. The information they have is good, but presented in a bureaucratic rather than academic or personal manner. According to their website, "USCIRF is an independent, bipartisan U.S. federal government commission, the first of its kind in the world, dedicated to defending the universal right to freedom of religion or belief abroad. USCIRF reviews the facts and circumstances of religious freedom violations and makes policy recommendations to the President, the Secretary of State, and Congress. USCIRF Commissioners are appointed by the President and the Congressional leadership of both political parties." More information is available online at www.uscirf.gov.

U.S. Department of Justice Civil Rights Division: Part of the U.S. Department of Justice, and thus government-funded and subject to presidential policies and priorities. It is interesting to see how much or how little attention religious freedom and oppression issues receive in comparison to other "civil rights" priorities. Their website states, "The Civil Rights Division of the Department of Justice, created in 1957 by the enactment of the Civil Rights Act of 1957, works to uphold the civil and constitutional rights of all Americans, particularly some of the most vulnerable members of our society. The Division enforces federal statutes prohibiting discrimination on the basis of race, color, sex, disability, religion, familial status and national origin. Since its establishment, the Division has grown dramatically in both size and scope, and has played a role in many of the nation's pivotal civil rights battles." More information is available online at www.justice.gov/crt.

U.S. State Department Office of International Religious Freedom: Part of the U.S. Department of State, and thus government-funded and subject to presidential policies and priorities. It is interesting to see how much or how little attention religious freedom, oppression, and persecution issues receive in comparison to other State Department priorities.

According to their website, "the Office of International Religious Freedom has the mission of promoting religious freedom as a core objective of U.S. foreign policy. The office is headed by the Ambassador-at-Large for International Religious Freedom. . . . We monitor religious persecution and discrimination worldwide, recommend and implement policies in respective regions or countries, and develop programs to promote religious freedom. More information is available online at www.state.gov/j/drl/irf.

News Reporting and Analysis
Organizations (in alphabetical order)

This second set of resources is a list of news organizations where (depending on the style of reporting) you can find current articles, analysis, reports, and editorial pieces about religious freedom, persecution, policy issues, and related matters. Some of these organizations focus mainly on religious matters, while others include religious and religious freedom articles as part of a much wider scope of coverage. Some report from a Christian perspective, while others are clearly secular. However, the breadth of coverage reflected in this list provides a richness and authenticity that is worth perusing. As you scan through the materials, you will find that each organization has its own strengths, perspectives, and limitations. Several of them require subscriptions for full access, but you can probably find them at your local library and then decide if you would like to subscribe. Others offer enough information on their free websites to be worthwhile without any subscription. You may want to check more than one resource, and on a regular basis, to really stay abreast of developments and their implications.

Some news organizations are not on the list because they tend to avoid reporting on hostility toward Christians or because when they do report, they distort the facts by portraying a persecution problem as economic, political, or even environmental, avoiding the religious side of the news story entirely. This is their editorial choice to make, as it is also their decision whether to even mention an event at all. On the other hand, we in the United States are fortunate to have a wide range of domestic and international sources of reporting at our disposal, and many of them are very good. So if you have a favorite that did not make the list below, enjoy it anyway! You still might want to check out the options, though, in case one of them becomes a new favorite.

The American Interest	www.the-american-interest.com
Christianity Today	www.christianitytoday.com
The Economist	www.economist.com
The Federalist	www.thefederalist.com
The Wall Street Journal	www.wsj.com
World News Group	www.worldmag.com

Resources Available from The Lutheran Church—Missouri Synod

The following resources can be found by searching lcms.org:

- "Free to Be Faithful" (newsletter)

- Webinars on church and society issues

- LCMS and Amicus Curiae briefs

The Synod's Commission on Theology and Church Relations has several documents available for free at lcms.org/ctcr. See especially the following:

- *Why Are You Persecuting Me? A Christian Response to Hostility and Persecution* (2014)—good introductory study on the theological background for understanding persecution

- *Guidelines for Participation in Civic Events* (2004)—provides context that might be useful when working with other groups in common cause

- *The Bible and Christian Citizenship* (1996)—useful perspective on understanding our civil rights and responsibilities

- *Render Unto Caesar . . . and Unto God: A Lutheran View of Church and State* (1994)—helpful for participating in the political process and avoiding the extremes of either leaving the playing field or becoming too political

Appendix 2
Prayers for Those Facing Hostility and Persecution

It can be hard to know how to pray or what to pray when we or people we care about face hostility or persecution. Difficulties might arise either because the situation is so new to us or because the urgency of the circumstances prevents us from having much time to think or prepare. In either case, it may be helpful to refer to prayers others have prayed in such challenging situations.

Here are some example prayers from *Lutheran Service Book: Pastoral Care Companion* (St. Louis: Concordia, 2007), pages 532–33:

> Lord Jesus Christ, before whom all in heaven and earth shall bow, grant courage that I may confess Your saving name in the face of any opposition from a world hostile to the Gospel. Help me to remember the long line of Your faithful witnesses who endured persecution and even faced death rather than dishonor You. By Your Spirit, strengthen me to confess You before all, knowing the You will confess my name before Your Father in heaven; for You live and reign with the Father and the Holy Spirit, one God, now and forever.

Almighty God, Your Son, Jesus Christ, chose to suffer pain before going up to joy and crucifixion before entering into glory. Mercifully grant that I, walking in the way of the cross, may find this path to be the way of life and peace; through Jesus Christ, our Lord, who lives and reigns with You and the Holy Spirit, one God, now and forever.

Almighty, everlasting God, through Your only Son, our blessed Lord, You commanded us to love our enemies, to do good to those who hate us, and to pray for those who persecute us. Therefore, we earnestly implore You that by Your gracious working our enemies may be led to true repentance, may have the same love toward us as we have toward them, and may be of one accord and of one mind and heart with us and with Your whole Church; through Jesus Christ, our Lord, who lives and reigns with You and the Holy Spirit, one God, now and forever.

Some of the writers of the Psalms endured situations that might be as challenging as ours, or even more so. The Psalms record conversations with God that include pleas for help or rescue; expressions of anger, fear, frustration, and other emotions; and thanksgiving and praise for God's faithfulness and salvation. Here are a few psalms that might be useful as patterns or examples for our prayers.

Psalm 31:9–16, 19–20

Be gracious to me, O Lord, for I am in distress;
　　my eye is wasted from grief;
　　my soul and my body also.
For my life is spent with sorrow,
　　and my years with sighing;
my strength fails because of my iniquity,
　　and my bones waste away.

Because of all my adversaries I have become a reproach,
　　especially to my neighbors,

and an object of dread to my acquaintances;
    those who see me in the street flee from me.
I have been forgotten like one who is dead;
    I have become like a broken vessel.
For I hear the whispering of many—
    terror on every side!—
as they scheme together against me,
    as they plot to take my life.

But I trust in You, O LORD;
    I say, "You are my God."
My times are in Your hand;
    rescue me from the hand of my enemies
    and from my persecutors!
Make Your face shine on Your servant;
    save me in Your steadfast love!

Oh, how abundant is Your goodness,
    which You have stored up for those who fear You
and worked for those who take refuge in You,
    in the sight of the children of mankind!
In the cover of Your presence You hide them
    from the plots of men;
You store them in Your shelter
    from the strife of tongues.

Psalm 54

O God, save me by Your name,
    and vindicate me by Your might.
O God, hear my prayer;
    give ear to the words of my mouth.
For strangers have risen against me;
    ruthless men seek my life;
    they do not set God before themselves.

Behold, God is my helper;
    the Lord is the upholder of my life.
He will return the evil to my enemies;
    in Your faithfulness put an end to them.

With a freewill offering I will sacrifice to You;
    I will give thanks to Your name, O LORD, for it is good.
For He has delivered me from every trouble,
    and my eye has looked in triumph on my enemies.

Psalm 69:6–18

Let not those who hope in You be put to shame through me,
    O Lord GOD of hosts;
let not those who seek You be brought to dishonor
    through me,
    O God of Israel.
For it is for Your sake that I have borne reproach,
    that dishonor has covered my face.
I have become a stranger to my brothers,
    an alien to my mother's sons.

For zeal for Your house has consumed me,
    and the reproaches of those who reproach
    You have fallen on me.
When I wept and humbled my soul with fasting,
    it became my reproach.
When I made sackcloth my clothing,
    I became a byword to them.
I am the talk of those who sit in the gate,
    and the drunkards make songs about me.

But as for me, my prayer is to You, O LORD.
    At an acceptable time, O God, in the abundance of Your
    steadfast love answer me in your saving faithfulness.
Deliver me
    from sinking in the mire;
let me be delivered from my enemies
    and from the deep waters.
Let not the flood sweep over me,
    or the deep swallow me up,
    or the pit close its mouth over me.

Answer me, O Lord, for Your steadfast love is good;
according to Your abundant mercy, turn to me.
Hide not Your face from Your servant;
for I am in distress; make haste to answer me.
Draw near to my soul, redeem me;
ransom me because of my enemies!

Additional Helpful References:

Psalm 35	Psalm 71
Psalm 119:81–88	Psalm 143

Appendix 3
Quick Guide to Warnings and Promises in Scripture

The Bible cautions Christians that we will face hostility, oppression, or persecution, and often these words of warning come hand in hand with words of promise and encouragement. Many of these warnings and promises turn up in the words of Jesus, as recorded in the Gospels, while others come to light in apostolic letters to the early churches. If we cast our gaze farther, we find words of encouragement in the Psalms and in case studies discussed in chapter 3 (pp. 103–8) of this book.

The lists that follow provide references for many of the key passages of Scripture that warn of hostility or that provide encouragement for us in such times of difficulty. This list focuses on passages from the New Testament, which typically speaks to the Church and to disciples of Jesus Christ. You might find it helpful to peruse the list and then pick out one or two passages from God's Word that speak most directly to your situation and your heart.

Blessings on your journey!

Words of Warning

Matthew 10:16–25 Behold, I am sending you out as sheep in the midst of wolves, so be wise as serpents and innocent as doves. Beware of men, for they will deliver you over to courts and flog you in their synagogues, and you will be dragged before governors and kings for My sake, to bear witness before them and the Gentiles. When they deliver you over, do not be anxious how you are to speak or what you are to say, for what you are to say will be given to you in that hour. For it is not you who speak, but the Spirit of your Father speaking through you. Brother will deliver brother over to death, and the father his child, and children will rise against parents and have them put to death, and you will be hated by all for My name's sake. But the one who endures to the end will be saved. When they persecute you in one town, flee to the next, for truly, I say to you, you will not have gone through all the towns of Israel before the Son of Man comes. A disciple is not above his teacher, nor a servant above his master. It is enough for the disciple to be like his teacher, and the servant like his master. If they have called the master of the house Beelzebul, how much more will they malign those of his household.

⌘⌘

Matthew 16:24–26 Jesus told His disciples, "If anyone would come after Me, let him deny himself and take up his cross and follow Me. For whoever would save his life will lose it, but whoever loses his life for My sake will find it. For what will it profit a man if he gains the whole world and forfeits his soul? Or what shall a man give in return for his soul?"

⌘⌘

Matthew 24:9–13 Then they will deliver you up to tribulation and put you to death, and you will be hated by all nations for My name's sake. And then many will fall away and betray one another and hate one another. And many false prophets will arise and lead many astray. And because lawlessness will be increased, the love of many will grow cold. But the one who endures to the end will be saved.

⌘⌘

Mark 13:9 But be on your guard. For they will deliver you over to councils, and you will be beaten in synagogues, and you will stand before governors and kings for My sake, to bear witness before them.

⌘⌘

John 15:18–24 If the world hates you, know that it has hated Me before it hated you. If you were of the world, the world would love you as its own; but because you are not of the world, but I chose you out of the world, therefore the world hates you. Remember the word that I said to you: "A servant is not greater than his master." If they persecuted Me, they will also persecute you. If they kept My word, they will also keep yours. But all these things they will do to you on account of My name, because they do not know Him who sent Me. If I had not come and spoken to them, they would not have been guilty of sin, but now they have no excuse for their sin. Whoever hates Me hates My Father also. If I had not done among them the works that no one else did, they would not be guilty of sin, but now they have seen and hated both Me and My Father.

⌘⌘

1 Corinthians 16:13 Be watchful, stand firm in the faith, act like men, be strong.

⌘⌘

2 Timothy 4:3–4 For the time is coming when people will not endure sound teaching, but having itching ears they will accumulate for themselves teachers to suit their own passions, and will turn away from listening to the truth and wander off into myths.

⌘⌘

1 Peter 1:6–7 In this you rejoice, though now for a little while, if necessary, you have been grieved by various trials, so that the tested genuineness of your faith—more precious than gold that perishes though it is tested by fire—may be found to result in praise and glory and honor at the revelation of Jesus Christ.

⌘⌘

1 Peter 3:13–17 Now who is there to harm you if you are zealous for what is good? But even if you should suffer for righteousness' sake, you will be blessed. Have no fear of them, nor be troubled, but in your hearts honor Christ the Lord as holy, always being prepared to make a defense to anyone who asks you for a reason for the hope that is in you; yet do it with gentleness and respect, having a good conscience, so that, when you are slandered, those who revile your good behavior in Christ may be put to shame. For it is better to suffer for doing good, if that should be God's will, than for doing evil.

⌘⌘

1 Peter 4:12–16 Beloved, do not be surprised at the fiery trial when it comes upon you to test you, as though something strange were happening to you. But rejoice insofar as you share Christ's sufferings, that you may also rejoice and be glad when His glory is revealed. If you are insulted for the name of Christ, you are blessed, because the Spirit of glory and of God rests upon you. But let none of you suffer as a murderer or a thief or an evildoer or as a meddler. Yet if anyone suffers as a Christian, let him not be ashamed, but let him glorify God in that name.

⌘⌘

1 Peter 5:8–9 Be sober-minded; be watchful. Your adversary the devil prowls around like a roaring lion, seeking someone to devour. Resist him, firm in your faith, knowing that the same kinds of suffering are being experienced by your brotherhood throughout the world.

⌘⌘

Words of Promise

Matthew 5:10–12 Blessed are those who are persecuted for righteousness' sake, for theirs is the kingdom of heaven. Blessed are you when others revile you and persecute you and utter all kinds of evil against you falsely on My account. Rejoice and be glad, for your reward is great in heaven, for so they persecuted the prophets who were before you.

⌘⌘

Matthew 10:19–20 When they deliver you over, do not be anxious how you are to speak or what you are to say, for what you are to say will be given to you in that hour. For it is not you who speak, but the Spirit of your Father speaking through you.

⌘⌘

Matthew 16:24–26 Then Jesus told His disciples, "If anyone would come after Me, let him deny himself and take up his cross and follow Me. For whoever would save his life will lose it, but whoever loses his life for My sake will find it. For what will it profit a man if he gains the whole world and forfeits his soul? Or what shall a man give in return for his soul?"

⌘⌘

Matthew 28:18–20 Jesus came and said to them, "All authority in heaven and on earth has been given to Me. Go therefore and make disciples of all nations, baptizing them in the name of the Father and of the Son and of the Holy Spirit, teaching them to observe all that I have commanded you. And behold, I am with you always, to the end of the age."

⌘⌘

John 14:16–17 I will ask the Father, and He will give you another Helper, to be with you forever, even the Spirit of truth, whom the world cannot receive, because it neither sees Him nor knows Him. You know Him, for He dwells with you and will be in you.

⌘⌘

Romans 5:3–5 We rejoice in our sufferings, knowing that suffering produces endurance, and endurance produces character, and character produces hope, and hope does not put us to shame, because God's love has been poured into our hearts through the Holy Spirit who has been given to us.

⌘⌘

Romans 8:35–39 Who shall separate us from the love of Christ? Shall tribulation, or distress, or persecution, or famine, or nakedness, or danger, or sword? As it is written, "For Your sake we are being killed all the day long; we are regarded as sheep to be slaughtered." No, in all these things we are more than conquerors through Him who loved us. For I am sure that neither death nor life, nor angels nor rulers, nor things present nor things to come, nor powers, nor height nor depth, nor anything else in all creation, will be able to separate us from the love of God in Christ Jesus our Lord.

⌘⌘

1 Corinthians 12:26–27 If one member suffers, all suffer together; if one member is honored, all rejoice together. Now you are the body of Christ and individually members of it.

⌘⌘

2 Corinthians 1:3–7 Blessed be the God and Father of our Lord Jesus Christ, the Father of mercies and God of all comfort, who comforts us in all our affliction, so that we may be able to comfort those who are in any affliction, with the comfort with which we ourselves are comforted by God. For as we share abundantly in Christ's sufferings, so through Christ we share abundantly in comfort too. If we are afflicted, it is for your comfort and salvation; and if we are comforted, it is for your comfort, which you experience when you patiently endure the same sufferings that we suffer. Our hope for you is unshaken, for we know that as you share in our sufferings, you will also share in our comfort.

⌘⌘

2 Corinthians 4:7–10 But we have this treasure in jars of clay, to show that the surpassing power belongs to God and not to us. We are afflicted in every way, but not crushed; perplexed, but not driven to despair; persecuted, but not forsaken; struck down, but not destroyed; always carrying in the body the death of Jesus, so that the life of Jesus may also be manifested in our bodies.

⌘⌘

2 Corinthians 5:18–20b All this is from God, who through Christ reconciled us to Himself and gave us the ministry of reconciliation; that is, in Christ God was reconciling the world to Himself, not counting their trespasses against them, and entrusting to us the message of reconciliation. Therefore, we are ambassadors for Christ, God making His appeal through us.

⌘⌘

Ephesians 6:10–18 Finally, be strong in the Lord and in the strength of His might. Put on the whole armor of God, that you may be able to stand against the schemes of the devil. For we do not wrestle against flesh and blood, but against the rulers, against the authorities, against the cosmic powers over this present darkness, against the spiritual forces of evil in the heavenly places. Therefore take up the whole armor of God, that you may be able to withstand in the evil day, and having done all, to stand firm. Stand therefore, having fastened on the belt of truth, and having put on the breastplate of righteousness, and, as shoes for your feet, having put on the readiness given by the gospel of peace. In all circumstances take up the shield of faith, with which you can extinguish all the flaming darts of the evil one; and take the helmet of salvation, and the sword of the Spirit, which is the word of God, praying at all times in the Spirit, with all prayer and supplication. To that end keep alert with all perseverance, making supplication for all the saints.

⌘⌘

Philippians 3:7–14 But whatever gain I had, I counted as loss for the sake of Christ. Indeed, I count everything as loss because of the surpassing worth of knowing Christ Jesus my Lord. For His sake I have suffered the loss of all things and count them as rubbish, in order that I may gain Christ and be found in Him, not having a righteousness of my own that comes from the law, but that which comes through faith in Christ, the righteousness from God that depends on faith—that I may know Him and the power of His resurrection, and may share His sufferings, becoming like Him in His death, that by any means possible I may attain the resurrection from the dead. Not that I have already obtained this or am already perfect, but I press on to make it my own, because Christ Jesus has made me His own. Brothers, I do not consider that I have made it my own. But one thing I do: forgetting what lies behind and straining forward to what lies ahead, I press on toward the goal for the prize of the upward call of God in Christ Jesus.

⌘⌘

1 Timothy 2:1–4 First of all, then, I urge that supplications, prayers, intercessions, and thanksgivings be made for all people, for kings and all who are in high positions, that we may lead a peaceful and quiet life, godly and dignified in every way. This is good, and it is pleasing in the sight of God our Savior, who desires all people to be saved and to come to the knowledge of the truth.

⌘⌘

1 Peter 2:9–10 But you are a chosen race, a royal priesthood, a holy nation, a people for His own possession, that you may proclaim the excellencies of Him who called you out of darkness into His marvelous light. Once you were not a people, but now you are God's people; once you had not received mercy, but now you have received mercy.

⌘⌘

1 Peter 4:12–14 Beloved, do not be surprised at the fiery trial when it comes upon you to test you, as though something strange were happening to you. But rejoice insofar as you share Christ's sufferings, that you may also rejoice and be glad when His glory is revealed. If you are insulted for the name of Christ, you are blessed, because the Spirit of glory and of God rests upon you.

⌘⌘

Hebrews 1:1–3 Long ago, at many times and in many ways, God spoke to our fathers by the prophets, but in these last days He has spoken to us by His Son, whom He appointed the heir of all things, through whom also He created the world. He is the radiance of the glory of God and the exact imprint of His nature, and He upholds the universe by the word of His power. After making purification for sins, He sat down at the right hand of the Majesty on high.

⌘⌘

For a free downloadable Bible Study
and Discussion Guide,
visit *cph.org/standingfirm.*